PAPER DOLL

PAPER DOLL

Notes from a Late Bloomer

DYLAN MULVANEY

ABRAMS IMAGE, NEW YORK

Editor: Sarah Robbins
Designer: Diane Shaw
Managing Editor: Lisa Silverman
Production Manager: Sarah Masterson Hally

Library of Congress Control Number: 2024942528

ISBN: 978-1-4197-7039-5
eISBN: 979-8-88707-125-1
Signed edition ISBN: 978-1-4197-8590-0

Printed and bound in the United States
10 9 8 7 6 5 4 3 2 1

Some names and characteristics have been altered for privacy. Some
dialogue has been re-created. Neither the publisher nor the author
are responsible for or endorsing any specific resource in the back of
the book. Ayahuasca is a Schedule I illegal drug under US federal law,
and neither the publisher nor the author is endorsing its usage.

Abrams Image books are available at special discounts when purchased
in quantity for premiums and promotions as well as fundraising or
educational use. Special editions can also be created to specification. For
details, contact specialsales@abramsbooks.com or the address below.

Abrams Image® is a registered trademark of Harry N. Abrams, Inc.

ABRAMS The Art of Books
195 Broadway, New York, NY 10007
abramsbooks.com

For Lily,
the girl who helped show me the way

A LETTER TO YOU FROM ME

... is this a good time?

> Okay, good.

> Hi.

When I first dreamed of writing this book, I assumed it would be a fun, camp look into the first 365 days of my gender journey. I started journaling about my experiences and felt on top of the world. But shortly after my first year of transitioning, my shit got rocked. So, I had three options:

A) Send in the pretty pages I once planned for you.

B) Start from scratch and write a Shakespearean tragedy of the dramatic turn of events.

C) All of the above!

When I started my *Days of Girlhood* series on TikTok, I decided to show the good and the bad; the pretty and the raw; the ups and the downs of transition. I want to do the same thing with this book. These pages contain everything I didn't say on the internet and then some. This book is the most authentic version of myself—she's messy! This messiness includes mental health struggles, sexual trauma, and some heavy topics, so please read with care. Phew! Courageous conversation done. Now, I want to give you a little direction on how to navigate her.

How to Read *Paper Doll* Without Wanting to Pull Your Hair Out:

- The book follows two different timelines: my first 365 days of transitioning, and post-Beergate. If the section is in journal format, that means it happened within the first year, 2022-2023. If it's in essay format, that means it happened in the years before and/or after.

- Know that it is just my own personal transition journey and timeline. I am a baby trans, relatively new to this community. My story should never be used as the baseline or common experience of all trans people. Take any of my transition tools with a grain of salt—there is no right or wrong way, and isn't that gorgeous?

- While we're at it, I want to remind us all that there are soooo many different versions of girlhood and womanhood. And while this book focuses on mine, I honor them all.

- I write like I talk, so to my grammar policemen and -women and -humans out there, I apologize in advance. Shhh, just let it happen. Hehe.

- I want you to read this book in your cutest pajamas, way past your bedtime, with multiple beverages on your nightstand. If you're

listening to it, I want road trip, windows down,
hair blowing in the wind, full glam fantasy
vibes. Or while folding laundry works too.

- Pass this book along to a queen in your life who
  you think could use it. Even if it's a stranger
  who you can just sense has cute taste. Or be
  selfish and keep it for pink home décor!

- I never thought I would ever get to write a book,
  let alone have it published, so crazy dreams are
  possible. While reading this book, I want you to
  dream like CRAZY. Let your imagination go wild!!!

- I need you to believe sweet earnestness still exists.
  As I get older, I feel myself getting more cynical,
  and when I read back on my early transition days, it
  reminds me of the innocence I once allowed myself.
  The fight to remain sweetly earnest as we age just
  might be the greatest fight of all.

Okay, I think that's everything. Oh god, am I allowed
to end on eight? Lists usually end on ten, right?
Well, I did say this book would be unconventional,
so let's end with eight. And how nice for eight,
she finally gets her moment. Happy reading!

LOVE YA,

Dylan

THE
FALL OUT

am sitting on my porch in my tie-dye cat muumuu, smoking my first cigarette in years. I feel wildly guilty about having a smoke, but it's a thin Capri which makes the aesthetic a little bit cuter. A healthier cigarette . . . I think. The paparazzi that've been staking out my front yard for the last few weeks can't see me from behind the tall hedges, but I kind of wish they could just for this moment. How easy it'd be to throw the Disney-fied version of myself to the wind. I could see the headlines now: "Controversial Trans Influencer Dylan Mulvaney Crumbles Under Criticism, Picks Up Smoking and God Knows What Else." The shitty speakers on my phone are playing "Flightless Bird" from the *Twilight* soundtrack. This song is the only thing that's making me feel something. A notification pops up. It's Lily. "How r u? How's your heart?" A pinch of happiness to hear from my best friend. She just moved five thousand miles away but is still thinking of me, and then the sadness hits—she just moved five thousand miles away. How am I? People keep asking me that, and honestly, I don't know how to respond. I've always been very good about articulating how I'm feeling, but right now, at this moment, I don't know what to say other than "I don't think I'm doing so great." The song ends. I start to text back "I don't think I'm doing . . ." I change my mind. I don't want to worry Lily, so I just say, "Okay-ish. Just missing you." I look at the glowing orb of my half-finished cigarette. I hear my mom in my head, scolding me about lung cancer. I stub out the cute little half-Capri in the heart-shaped bowl I bought to fill with candy, now holding ashes. I take one last look at the hedges and go back inside the house. Cue: "Landslide."

DAY 1 of being a girl . . .

. . . And I'm coming out for the third time in my life today. The first time, I was fourteen and I came out as a gay boy, next was age twenty-four as nonbinary, and now, here I am at twenty-five, finally ready to tell the world that I am a trans woman. AH!

I've already been on hormones now for a few months, and I've had sit-downs with my close friends and family, but I'm breakin' the news to everyone else. I'm coming out on a Friday so that I can hide this weekend, and it also gives the girls from my hometown a hot topic to dish on at Sunday brunch. This has been a long, longgggg time coming.

A Conversation with My Mom When I Was Four

Four-year-old me: Mom!

Mom: Yes?

Four-year-old me: I think God made a mistake.

Mom: What do you mean?

Four-year-old me: I think he put a girl in a boy's body.

Mom: Oh, God doesn't make mistakes. You are perfect the way you are.

And that was that. No shade to Mom; it was the year 2000 and resources were limited for trans youth, especially living in a conservative household.

After over twenty years of ignoring the Angel of Transness tapping on my shoulder, telling me that I'm a woman, I couldn't ignore her anymore. Last night, I put barrettes in my hair and chicken cutlets in my top, and made a seven-minute heartfelt coming-out video to post on social media.

I think coming-out videos aren't as necessary
these days (gen z seems to have less shame and more
confidence), but I'm on the millennial cusp, so I grew
up in a time when novel-length coming-out Facebook
proclamations and teary-eyed YouTube confessionals
reigned supreme. My coming-outs were partly
theatrical and partly apologetic, and today's was no
different. The theatrical part is from my musical
theater degree. The apologetic part is from my Catholic
guilt. I even wrote out everything I wanted to say
on my computer first so that I made sure I got every
single point in. I did shed some tears while filming.
Tears of happiness. Grief. Release. This was by far the
scariest one I've ever done, and hopefully the last.
But I can't live another day of being misgendered
when I know so firmly who I am. I'm hoping this all
doesn't come as too much of a shock to the people who
know me (I mean, they have already seen me change
pronouns once before), but this is still major.

I uploaded the emotionally taxing video, watched it
back, and cringed. *God, Dylan, why so dramatic?!*
I've been doing stand-up for a few months now, so
I figured, why not put my comedy chops to use and
make a satirical video to lighten the mood.

I originally planned to start my transition in private,
but that felt like putting my life on pause. I don't really
know how this will go over, but it feels nice to find the
funny . . . Dylan, please always look for the funny.

The world sees you as a man in a dress.

You should've gone into hiding.

The girls at brunch are laughing at you.

Publicly sharing my transition could be a massive failure. And now for our regularly scheduled programming of DYLAN'S! DARK! THOUGHTS! Dylan's Dark Thoughts has been a recurring segment in my life since my early teen years. Let's take a look at what they have to say today.

I open my phone and the first few comments on the video are sweet and supportive. Take that, Dark Thoughts! Okay, for now, sharing it with others feels nice.

I'm really proud of you, Dylan. Terrified, and proud. Here's to showing the good, the bad, and the ugly. I think we deserve some Domino's deep pan pizza tonight.

LOVE YA,

Dylan

DAY 2 of being a girl . . .

. . . And women hate me. Let me rephrase that: The
women of TikTok hate me. Making an apology video
on Day 2 wasn't exactly what I had planned,
but here we are. My Day 1 video is getting a lot of
traction in a bad way. I woke up to 500,000 views
and thousands of comments debating my right to
womanhood. Being controversial goes against all the
people-pleasing skills I've developed since childhood.
Did I just ruin everything with one video?

I thought I was being relatable, but here's a bunch
of ladies in my comments saying I will never be a
woman, that they are deeply offended, and that my
stubble is showing. I just want to curl into a ball
and never unfurl. I don't know what to do other
than make an apology video.

Okay, I'm just going to apologize so these ladies know
that I'm not a threat. I feel terrible. The group I want to
be accepted by the most is the one that wants nothing
to do with me. Growing up gay, and then a brief chapter of
nonbinary, I had wonderful friendships and connections
with women. They are my safe space. But it feels like
something just . . . shifted. The women of TikTok
plucked me out of the "twinky gay friend" box, took
one good look at me, and said, *We don't claim her.* Oof.

Luckily, one of my best friends, Keesh, is in town, and we're going to the Rose Bowl Flea Market for vintage shopping. Shopping is an excellent distraction from the Dark Thoughts.

When Keesh shows up at my apartment, I instantly feel better. Her bright pink hair and warmer-than-the-sun smile put me at ease. Keesh is a sheepherder, registered nurse, meditation instructor—just to name a few of her part-time careers—so she knows how to comfort those in need. I first met Keesh

Her name is Loraine, but I call her Keesh, like quiche Lorraine.

when I was six years old. Her daughter Mae and I took acting classes together, and while Mae and I were friends too, I've always been the kind of kid who really connects with moms. (At pool parties growing up, you'd find me with my legs crossed, sipping a Capri-Sun like it was a Cosmo all while dishing the hottest goss with the moms in the kitchen.) Later, in my teen years, Keesh and I reconnected when Mae and I were in a production of *Legally Blonde* together. Keesh and I continued finding each other over and over again. When I couldn't ignore the Angel of Transness anymore, Keesh is who I went to. She is the woman I emulated; I wore the same bright, chunky knits (the clothes were literally hers) and styled my hair in pigtail braids just like hers.

Keesh is the perfect distraction from the angry internet; she is safety, she is home. But I can still feel the comments section seizing up in my pocket, and it's eating away at me. I could puke from nerves. I must fix this. All I ever wanted was to connect with other women, and the desire to be liked by them is outweighing my desire to put the phone down. Maybe they just need to see more parts of my personality! Maybe if I make a few more videos, they'll see what I am really like. As soon as I stepped into the flea market, I turned the camera on and hit record.

As I wandered through the parking lot pop-up booths, I filmed some of my favorite finds. I scored some great vintage dresses to add to my wardrobe too. Most trans gals have to start completely fresh, but luckily I had been wearing women's clothes (mostly Keesh's) for the past year while identifying as nonbinary, so my closet is already a work in progress.

Half my closet is new and feminine, and the other half, the more masculine side, has been sitting there gathering dust. Now that I am stepping into my joy, I don't want to keep the clothing that I wore during boyhood. But what if I need something boyish-looking for an audition? God, I hope I don't have to keep going in for male roles. The last part I played was a Mormon boy, Elder White, in the Broadway musical tour of *The Book of Mormon*, and I have no interest in playing that again. The nonbinary roles I auditioned for were equally off; every nonbinary character had a nose

ring and a shaved head, and was named after a type of tree. Oof. There are no characters that fit who I truly am, and I fear that no one will cast me to play female characters. It might take a while for the industry to know what to do with me. Even TikTok is having a complete meltdown over the fact that I'm a girl.

The Rose Bowl was nice, but I still couldn't shake the stress of feeling like the whole internet was mad at me, so Keesh and I went to one of my all-time favorite places on earth: the Grove. I love the Grove. It's this big, obnoxious outdoor mall in the middle of Los Angeles. There are trolleys and palm trees and high-end stores where I can go spend money on things I don't necessarily need but might make me feel better. It's a clean, manicured escape from the real world. Disneyland for adults. Oh, and of course, we can't forget Wetzel's Pretzels. I can't go to a mall and not get Wetzel's. It's a must. Feel free to sub it for Auntie Anne's depending on where you're geograph- ically located. Even though I was at the Grove, with all of its carb-y distractions, I couldn't help but keep checking my phone. I had some sort of addictive impulse to read every single comment. Luckily, Keesh was equally fascinated with the virality, which is good because I wasn't fully present with her or the Grove, just doomscrolling every five seconds.

The hundreds of comments were sending me into paralysis. But I somehow mustered the courage to edit and post the Day 2 video. As soon as it was uploaded, I sat in bed and cried. Then that crying turned into sobbing. Then came the Dark Thoughts.

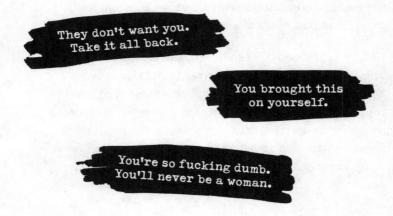

Maybe you'll get lucky and an asteroid will hit your WeHo apartment, and that way you don't have to handle it yourself. You don't really want to be here.

I could call a friend, Keesh maybe, but the Dark Thoughts convince me that she doesn't want to talk to me.

No one wants to talk to you. No one wants to be your friend.

The most alarming shift in today's Dark Thoughts is that they echo the comments section of my last two posts. The Dark Thoughts now have user names and avatars.

I can't tell the difference between my own Dark Thoughts and the angry comments section anymore. The Angel of Transness provides a moment of reprieve, reminding me that just yesterday, I saw my gender and transition so clearly with validation from doctors and loved ones alike. But with this many external opinions, the Dark Thoughts win.

Maybe everything you've felt about your gender is actually mental illness like they say it is. You've trusted women your entire life, why not believe them now?

I know loneliness well. Sometimes we're even BFF's. But right now, she's a real bitch, and I'm worried I'll get trapped in her clutches forever. The one thing I love about sobbing is how tired it makes me. I can't act on anything. Too sleepy. The Dark Thoughts can pick up where they left off in the morning.

You don't deserve a Domino's deep pan pizza tonight.

GOOD NIGHT,

Dylan

DAY 3 of being a girl . . .

. . . AND NOT ALL WOMEN HATE ME!!! THANK YOU, GOD! I woke up today expecting to welcome the Dark Thoughts back with open arms, but I refreshed the comments section, and boom. A cyber war.

Stop appropriating my gender.

Dylan can't appropriate being a girl because she is one.

Don't listen to these women, sweetie! I do all of those things frequently!

I was totally giggling until I went to the comments. Shame on all of you women for hating on her.

Y'all are a bunch of TERFs SMDH.

Seeing positive comments flood in, all from women of different ages, made me want to cry tears of relief. I have a lot of growing to do, which I'm well aware of and completely ready for, but I'm not trying to upset anyone here. But, wait, hold up . . . what's a

TERF?

Quick google.

TERF /tərf/ a trans-exclusionary radical feminist: an advocate of radical "feminism" who believes that a trans woman's gender identity is not legitimate and who is hostile to the inclusion of trans people and gender-diverse people in the feminist movement.

Ohhhhh! So, there are women who just hate *all* trans people, not just me? Good to know, good to know. The pieces are coming together. That's the other thing about me, I don't really know much of the trans terminology yet. I've probably met fewer than five trans people in my life (at least that I'm aware of), and I hadn't even heard the term *nonbinary* until two years ago. You'd think being part of the queer alphabet mafia that I'd be more in the know, but in the very white privileged spaces I've previously occupied, the letters often stay isolated from each other.

Well . . . at least I know what these catty women are now. TERFs! WOO! I spent the rest of my day watching WORLD WAR SHE unfold, with more supportive women adding in and eventually overpowering the haters. Okay, my Day 1 video must have ended up on the wrong side of the internet. Noted.

All of my content up until this point hasn't been seen as controversial. Animal videos. Singing Broadway covers. I thought I had a good handle on what it meant to go viral after a few of my other TikToks had taken off (Google: Dylan Mulvaney Bison), but this hit different. All the attention was . . . TERRIFYING.

I'm the kind of gal who lies awake at night when I suspect one person dislikes me, let alone thousands, hence the sobbing last night. I'm also the kind of gal who plots how to make said person like me no matter what it takes. This would be challenging given that there are now thousands of these TERF's and I don't know their addresses to send Edible Arrangements. So, making more *Days of Girlhood* videos is my best shot at winning them over.

Last night I was trapped in bed apologizing in the comments section. Tonight I'm in bed thanking all the kind women who left messages of support. This feels better than an apology tour. I changed "I'm sorry" to "thank you" and noticed something wild began to happen. These kind women in my comments were following me. Like . . . a lot. Whoa. Every few seconds a new name pops up in my notifications followed by a serotonin rush.

My obsessive refreshing of my notifications leaves no room for the Dark Thoughts to creep in. I refresh until my eyes burn.

LOVE YA,

Dylan

Chapter 1

THE UNTOUCHABLE "IT GIRL" SYNDROME

Let's get one thing straight: Before anything else, I'm a musical theater girl through and through. Which is why for my big Day 365 of Girlhood Celebration, I self-indulgently put on a musical staged retelling of my first year of transition. We filled the iconic Rainbow Room on the sixty-fifth floor of 30 Rockefeller Plaza with trans folks, celebs, and my closest loved ones. The show was a hit. We raised almost $200,000 for the Trevor Project. It was truly the most magical night of my life.

Needless to say, on day 366 of being a girl, I woke up hungover. Like "I texted 4 exes, lost my phone, and left my card at the bar" hungover. The Rainbow Room was the Charlotte York version of me, and the after-party was my Samantha Jones moment. I went all out and rented the Box, my all-time favorite club in New York City. The reason I love the Box so much is because you'll be in the middle of dancing on a table, then the lights will dim and everyone will immediately find a seat for their epically naughty shows. Performances can include anything from a woman spewing lava out of her vagina from the top of a papier-mâché volcano to burlesque dancers spinning naked from the ceiling by their ponytails. (Yay nudity!) For my party, we opted for the spinning ponytails. During the performance, the dancers brought me onstage to snort a giant pile of prop cocaine, aka powdered sugar. I was nervous someone would take their phone out and film a scandalous video, but the energy of Day 365 let my normal Good Girl precautions take the night off . . . I couldn't think of a better way to step out of my days of girlhood and into my life of womanhood than slamming champagne with two hundred of my wildest friends.

I wobbled home to the Plaza Hotel and curled up in bed next to Lily as the sun was coming up. As I closed my eyes, with the biggest smile on my face, my alarm went off. Fuck! I forgot I had to be in hair and makeup for a photoshoot with *Allure* magazine first thing in the morning. I tore out of bed, rinsed the rat's nest that was once a French twist out of my hair, and headed out the door to Condé Nast headquarters, where I immediately went into more hair.

Keesh, who flew in from the farm for my show, accompanied me to the photoshoot. She'd never been on a set like that before. It felt like both of my worlds were combining into something incredible; the woman who dressed me in my first female clothes was now watching me navigate designer labels and finding my best angles. It was sweet and symbolic, a full-circle moment where I found some semblance of the new normal. Keesh was following every person around in her motherly herding manner. Chatting up my publicist and asking questions about everyone's private life. Taking pictures of pictures. I love her so much.

While six different people were primping various parts of my body, I pulled away the free hand that wasn't getting a manicure and opened up TikTok, only to see that Lady Gaga had commented on my Day 365 Live opening number with: "This is brilliant!!😭" A flash of my thirteen-year-old self at her Monster Ball concert made me smile. I wonder what that kid would think of all of this now. The comment under hers said, "YOU ARE THE IT GIRL OF OUR GENERATION" with a bunch of little heart emojis. My mind was spinning.

How did I go from theater kid to IT Girl?

* * * * *

As a theater kid, when I envisioned what my career would look like, being a cover girl with enough followers to populate a small Mediterranean country was not at all what I imagined. I wanted to be Broadway-level famous: signing playbills at the stage door but not being recognized on the street, 10K followers on Instagram, performing in the Macy's Thanksgiving Day Parade for naysayers back in my hometown. To me that was the perfect level of fame. In some ways, I still think it is.

If you'll indulge me, let's take a walk down memory lane. When I was three years old, my parents took me to see *The Grinch* at the Old Globe Theater in San Diego. (Fun fact: Vanessa Hudgens played Cindy Lou!) The moment the orchestra hit that opening downbeat, my little three-year-old baby arm had chills. It was like I was being transported to another universe. One where everyone had smiles on their faces and were belting Christmas showtunes. There were both adults and kids onstage, and even at three, I was like, "Oh shit, wait, you're telling me KIDS can do that?" Still to this day, I have never had more FOMO in my entire life. During the first number, I turned to my mom and said, "I want to do this."

I've always been a 0 to 100 kind of person. And from then on, the only thing I could think about was getting up on that stage, so I harassed my mother to put me in dance lessons until she finally gave in. I enrolled at Diane's School of Dance and was the only boy in the entire school. If you were paying attention, you'll remember from page 6 that I came out as a girl to my mom right around this time. Since I couldn't live in my true identity, the next best thing was to do something that brought me an immense amount of joy, and that was dance. I absolutely loved everything about it.

You had to be six years old to audition for *The Grinch*. So, I spent the next three years in dance class. The second I hit six, I marched right into that audition and sang the most rousing version of "You're a Grand Old Flag" my little lungs would allow. Shockingly, I didn't book it. How unpatriotic of the casting team. This would be the first of my many disappointments in showbiz. I hadn't even considered this outcome. I was confused. But this is where my "glass-half-full" mentality started to develop. I thought to myself, *We'll get 'em next year!*

At seven years old, I went in with a less patriotic approach and belted out a crowd favorite: "Zip-a-Dee-Doo-Dah." Well, turns out it wasn't this crowd's favorite, because once again, I didn't book it. This time the casting team shared feedback with my mom that I should work on my singing skills. It was at this moment I realized that I spent the last four years in dance classes to get the part, when in reality, I should've been in voice lessons. *Damn it, Dylan! How could you have missed this?* I went back to the drawing board and took the next two years to work with a voice coach and audition for youth theater instead of trying to go straight to the big leagues. And thank God I didn't get my big break, because the first musical I booked was *High School Musical*, where I met my best friend and soulmate Lily Drew Detwiler. (For those interested, I played Ryan, the flamboyant sidekick, but we all *know* I'd be cast as Sharpay now. Lily is still bitter about being cast in the "Get'cha Head in the Game" basketball ensemble. We don't talk about this.)

Once I had some experience under my belt, at ten years old I auditioned for *The Grinch* for a third time. I sang "I Just Can't Wait to Be King," with full choreography AND arm movements timed to specific lyrics. I also had somewhat of a professional headshot that wasn't taken at the mall. I mean . . . I knocked it out of the park, but now—as we say in the biz—it was the waiting game.

That week, when my divorced parents showed up at my school with Martinelli's, I thought my prayers worked and they were getting back together, but nope! This was even better. They came together to tell me I had won the prized role of Danny Who (Cindy Lou Who's brother, for those who aren't familiar), and I would be starting rehearsals in just a few weeks. Who needs happily married parents? Danny Who doesn't!

Being in *The Grinch* was EVERYTHING to me. I walked into that theater like I was Beyoncé and this was my Homecoming Tour. *The Grinch* was also the first time I was around openly gay adult men. Seeing queer men flourish in theater, making money in a creative environment while outwardly expressing themselves, gave me hope. I spent Sundays at my mom's new-age Christian church listening to the pastor go on about how gay marriage was a sin, then I'd go to the theater and see these queer actors happy and thriving. Some of them even had life partners of twenty-plus years whom I got to meet, and I remember thinking, *Whoa . . . this would really piss off my pastor.* Being around incredible gay performers who were living authentically made me think, *If I can't be a girl, maybe being a gay boy in theater is the next best thing.* And so, my twinkdom was born.

I did *The Grinch* for three years, eventually graduating to the role of Teen Who because of my height, and started pursuing other professional gigs. My mom began driving me up to LA for auditions I'd receive from a kids' talent manager who spotted me in *High School Musical* and signed me shortly after. I always liked her because she had the exact tenacity of Joey's agent from *Friends*.

After one specific Disney Channel audition, the talent manager called my mom to say, "Tell Dylan to stop wearing makeup, the casting office complained." I jumped in: "I'M NOT WEARING MAKEUP!" (I was, in fact, wearing makeup.) I didn't get the part or any others. Whether it was the cakey orange foundation, my quickly sprouting height, or my limp wrists, I didn't end up on the Disney Channel child star track, so the industry would have to wait to really mess me up until my twenties. I did, however, book professional theater in San Diego, which was the original plan anyway.

I went to a high school where I could take free periods, so I'd show up in sweats at 8 a.m., put in a few hours of school, and then head to rehearsal. I did *Spring Awakening*, a musical in which I was to kiss an older actor onstage, so my mom asked if we could get an STD panel run on him due to her overwhelming fear that gay men are much more likely to contract something. I personally didn't see a stage kiss to HIV pipeline, so I shot that down fast.

After that, I got my first big lead in a show called *Bare: A Pop Opera*, where I played a Catholic schoolboy battling his queerness alongside his relationship to God. Sound familiar? No method acting necessary, I was already living that role. In that musical, there was a song between my character and his mother during which he came out. On opening night, my own mom audibly sobbed through the song, exclaiming, "That's me! That's me!" Lily held her hand through the whole second act.

With all these productions going on, my life in high school was less about being there and more about being done with it. Every time I was anywhere that wasn't rehearsal, I kept thinking, *I have to go back to my real life at the theater*, where my faggy, campy personality traits were not only tolerated but rewarded. I was a big fish in a small pond in San Diego, and for a brief moment I began to feel like I had "It." But that feeling disappeared when I decided to audition for theater programs at a college level.

Remember the 0 to 100 tendencies I developed as a three-year-old? They never left me. And at seventeen years old, my new *Grinch* became Juilliard. Back then, I was a major gleek, and I had heard that Rachel and Kurt's fictional college, NYADA, was based on the Juilliard School in New York City. I too wanted to follow in Kurt's footsteps and gallivant around Times Square singing songs from *Wicked*, because that's obviously how musical theater school in New York works.

Well, I had such a rude awakening when I was forced to audition with a Shakespeare monologue (NOT my strongest suit). I was immediately rejected at the first stage, before I could show the Juilliard professors my singing and dancing skillz. My dreams were crushed. It's since been revealed to me that this was a ridiculous dream because THEY DON'T EVEN TEACH MUSICAL THEATER AT JUILLIARD?! Oh well, if I'd been accepted, I would've been a nightmare trying to Fosse my way through Shakespeare.

The next best thing was the Cincinnati College-Conservatory of Music, one of the top arts conservatories in the country. My friend Hannah from *The Grinch* was a rising senior, so I flew to Ohio to spend welcome weekend with her and see if I had a future with CCM. Once on campus, my seventeen-year-old heart couldn't take it. GAY BOYS. MY OWN AGE. EVERYWHERE. They were hot AND knew all the words to the *Newsies* soundtrack. I immediately enrolled. My first few years were filled with beer pong and winning over the hearts of upperclassmen; a few of these hookups were the IT Boys of Musical Theater. Being around these IT Boys taught me more of what having "IT" meant.

* * * * *

To be an IT Boy in musical theater, you either have to be straight or a gay boy who is very masculine presenting. They all had muscles that could lift the girls in the dance numbers. IT Boys were often tall and walked with the swagger of a cowboy fresh off his horse.

In a sophomore-year batshit acting class, we even had a workshop for the gays to "Learn How to Walk Like a Straight Man." I didn't make it two steps before the teacher briskly excused me from the workshop—there was no hope for me. After this slightly embarrassing event, I recruited Frankie, the hottest straight guy in my class and #1 IT Boy on campus, to train me in the gym and to get . . . how do you say it? *Swole*. He recommended a mass weight gainer, which I tried for many months, but never was I able to gain an ounce of muscle. I think either my hyper-fast metabolism or my suspected tapeworm, Tammy, was working overtime to keep me small. No matter how much effort I put into being an acceptable version of a gay man, or how hard I tried to shed the feminine parts of myself, I could never touch the level of attention these IT Boys were getting. And attention is currency; in college, in theater, and in life. I was, however, friends with the IT Girls. The next best thing. Catch my drift?

Being friends with the IT Girls gave me a new level of protection and status. I didn't necessarily have a seat at the table, but I had a booster chair next to my roommate Bryn, Frankie's girlfriend and a resident IT Girl in her own right. The apartment Bryn and I shared was the cutest Pottery Barn shit you've ever seen. A whole vibe. We nicknamed it "The Fun Home" (IYKYK) and threw the best pregames this side of the Ohio River.

When senior year rolled around, there no longer were hot upperclassmen to chase, and since I've always preferred older men, I had more time to focus on my studies. During this more-focused era of college Dylan, one class changed everything for me: cabaret. In this class we were each expected to write and star in our own one-person shows. Mine was called *Gay in a Beret: A Cabaret*, a rousing retelling of my solo trip to Europe the summer before senior year. I rewrote lyrics to famous musicals and talked about my hookups. I wrote some of my first jokes and sang songs traditionally sung by women.

During my performance, my classmates' faces lit up, as if they were seeing me step into my power in real time, right in front of them. That was the first moment, and a fleeting one, that I got to experience what it felt like to be "IT" while at school . . . to have that X factor. I'd spent my life studying material someone else created, memorizing lines someone else wrote, trying to replicate a role someone else had played. For most of college I'd be cast in the ensemble, hoping for a small feature or solo, a chance to be noticed, but settling for the next best thing. And, honestly, that set me up for the industry brilliantly. Having low expectations? I can't recommend it enough. After performing *Gay in a Beret*, I began to think that maybe there was something to writing and performing my own material.

At the end of the year, my class arrived in New York City to perform our Senior Showcase for agents and casting directors. I didn't think I would be a hot commodity, so I just went with the goal of having as much fun as possible.

For my showcase, I picked two songs—one was this fabulous feminine number, "And You Don't Even Know It," from the UK musical *Everybody's Talking About Jamie*. It's a wildly confident and queer song that no one in the States had heard before.

> *So kiss my ass goodbye*
> *'Cause I'm gonna be the one*

The other was "(Just a) Simple Sponge" from *SpongeBob Square-Pants: The New Musical*. Gotta show range!

> *. . . there is more to me than just my name*
> *Give me a chance and I could change the game*

I was not . . . subtle.

After my showcase, I got thirteen offers for meetings from theater agents. I couldn't believe it. Sure, it wasn't as many as Frankie, but it still blew my mind in the best way.

Most of us musical theater majors moved to New York City with Broadway on the mind. My first audition in New York was for *The Book of Mormon*, and I was in luck because I'd auditioned for the show in LA when I was seventeen years old. Back then, I made it to the final callback but ultimately didn't get the role because I fucked up the tap dance combo baaad. The choreography was to one of my favorite songs in the musical theater canon, "Turn It Off."

> *Being gay is bad,*
> *but lying is worse*

I refused to let tap dancing, my mortal enemy, be the reason I lost out on my Broadway dreams. So, what did I do? I HUSTLED, BITCH! While in college, a ton of the alumni were in *The Book of*

Mormon, so I got them to send me the choreography on video and hired a tap teacher, Katie Jo, to drill "Turn It Off" with me for MONTHS. Katie Jo was one of the only faculty members at that school who made me feel like I had talent. Eventually, with her help, I could do the tap number in my sleep. When the audition came around again four years later, I had that shit on lock. If they asked me to do any other move than what I had been practicing, I would've been screwed, but as far as the casting team knew, I was the best tapper in the room!

A week later, my professor (who once told me junior year that my newly bleached blonde hair looked like "shit" and made me dye it back immediately) called to tell me he'd received a note from the casting agents asking if I was a good student in school. "A good sign," he told me over the phone. A week after that, my brand-new agent called to tell me that I booked it. I BOOKED IT!

Even though I was, once again, in the ensemble with just a few lines, and it was the national tour, not as prestigious as the New York production, I was more than okay with that. I was the first kid from my program to book a Broadway musical post-college, and I'm not going to lie, it felt gooooooood. **Cue: "Girl on Fire" by Alicia Keys.**

The show even pushed up my start date by a week when they realized I could make my debut in my hometown theater, the San Diego Civic Theatre. This meant I had only eight days to learn and rehearse a full three-hour musical. I had my debut, in front of three thousand people including my family, in the theater where I saw every Broadway musical growing up. I couldn't have written a better start to my adult career.

I was living like a SAINT at the beginning of the run, because I was scared that casting had made a mistake and were going to fire me once they found out I actually do not have IT. As the Tenor 1, I was singing high Bs and sometimes Cs, which is really hard on the vocal cords—so I gave up dairy, aka my main food group, and my version of a naughty treat at the end of a show was a Pamplemousse La Croix (carbonation isn't great for the cords either).

What followed was a whirlwind tour around the United States, as well as Mexico and Canada. The cast and I got closer and closer with each performance, and I became best friends with Alyah Chanelle Scott, the other twenty-two-year-old in the show. We called it our fifth year of college, because most of the time we had no idea what was going on, but we eventually learned how to party AND do eight shows a week. Alyah was clearly an IT Girl and played Nabulungi, the lead role; I'd watch her big number from offstage every night, marveling at her talent. When we brought the show to LA for a long sit-down engagement, Alyah and I started chatting about the possibility of moving to California permanently post-tour. She wanted to pursue TV and film acting (and she did it! She got a starring role in *The Sex Lives of College Girls.*), and I just liked the warm weather. One night backstage, Alyah told me about this app called TikTok. "I think you'd be really great at it—you could do comedy and tell stories!" The people around me kept telling me that I was really funny, but I never thought this skill would extend beyond epic cocktail party conversation.

I thought back to my *Gay in a Beret* days, how much I loved telling jokes to my classmates, and wondered if maybe I should try comedy. I signed up for a class at Upright Citizens Brigade and had set a meeting with a small LA theater agency when . . . Covid hit. Hard. The whole cast for sure got it in like February 2020—we were serving plague energy but would show up to the theater anyway like, "I have this weird cold!" A boy in the ensemble joked about the show shutting down, and I—possibly the most superstitious person you'll ever meet—screamed, "WHAT YOU SAY HAS POWER, DON'T SPEAK THAT INTO EXISTENCE! KNOCK ON WOOD!" The next morning, we got the call that *The Book of Mormon* was canceled for the rest of the LA run. I still blame you for not knocking on wood, Steven.

For the first time in my life, the show could not go on. So, I packed up all my stuff and drove down south to my dad's house. Like everyone else in the world, I figured it would all blow over in a couple of weeks. Ha.

Back in San Diego sitting at my dad's, in the same place I'd worked so hard to get out of, I had nothing to do but think. There were no costumes, or scripts, or fantasy worlds to disappear inside of. I could no longer hide behind the next best thing to cloak my discomfort. All I had was reality. And it was in this reality that all the thoughts and feelings and questions I'd been blanketing in performance came rising up to the surface. It was in this reality that I was able to find the best thing: my true identity.

It was obvious to me that I didn't feel like a boy, but I still wasn't ready to admit to myself that I was a girl, not in the way I did so freely as a four-year-old. During this time, I had nothing to do but scroll. Social media was my only connection to the world, and it's online that I saw that one of my older classmates from college, Elle, had come out as nonbinary. I hadn't even heard of the nonbinary identity until just weeks before, when I met someone named Fightmaster at a comedy show who uses they/them pronouns. And now a classmate of mine that I knew for so long on one end of the gender binary was also using they/them! I went down a Google rabbit hole, reading everything about being nonbinary. I started bargaining with myself: "Okay, if I don't feel like a boy, then maybe I should just creep off the binary to something closer to what I feel."

The next year of my life was truly transitional. I grew my hair. I took a soul-searching solo road trip across the country. My version of *Eat, Pray, Love* on a budget. I slowly came out to my family and friends as nonbinary, quietly adding he/they to my Instagram bio. Theater was still dead, and as I searched for any and all creative outlets, Alyah's recommendation re-entered the chat, so I started a TikTok account.

* * * * *

One morning, I opened my TikTok account and wanted to post something. I scrolled through my camera roll and found a cute, but old, video of me holding a koala. I made a joke about how the koala was gay and posted it. It got eight million views in a matter of forty-eight hours. My musical theater brain couldn't comprehend this type of exposure, trying to picture eight million people in the audience. Damn, that would have to be a big theater. The high I felt from the likes and comments wasn't as filling as applause, but at least I was eating. When the notifications went quiet, I felt back to square one. Am I supposed to make another one already? In theater, it can take years to produce a show, but on TikTok people were posting new things daily. TikTok loved the koala vid, so I thought I should try for more animal content.

While y'all were making bread, I was driving around America looking for more animals to pet and more videos to make during the pandemic. While in upstate Washington, basically Canada, I found a drive-through animal reserve called the Olympic Game Farm, where they give you a loaf of bread and send you through the park with little to no direction. I put my phone on the dash, pulled out my Bluetooth microphone from Amazon, and began recording myself feeding a baby dear. Suddenly, out of nowhere, a bison ran up and shoved his face INTO my car, resulting in one of the scariest, and most entertaining, moments of my life. When I get scared, I sing. So, I began to sing, "TAKEEE MY BREEEAD," in an opera voice, as if the melody would charm the bison out of my car. Luckily, I got the moment on camera. I uploaded to TikTok, and *boom*. Ten million views.

Once back in San Diego, I pondered on how to keep making animal content, because it's pretty hard to come by. BITCH! You live in San Diego! The San Diego Zoo, duh! So, I pitched my first ever project to the San Diego Zoo's social team, called *Interviewing Animals with Dylan*, where I'd chat with the animals like *Billy on the Street*, but with puns and sketch comedy. To my surprise, they said yes. I made multiple videos there until I ruffled some feathers: some conservationist higher-ups allegedly implied that I was humanizing the animals by talking to them as if they were people and that it was against their mission statement.

I was heartbroken, but it gave me the confidence to put myself out there. *The Ellen DeGeneres Show* had shared my bison video on their page, so I reached out to their socials team and said I'd like to do *Interviewing Animals* as a segment. Shockingly, they loved the idea. We started to shoot some content at different sanctuaries with a small budget and an even smaller crew (i.e., any friend who I could convince to tag along), but God was I having fun. This opportunity gave me the confidence to finally do the move to LA that Alyah and I talked about, with my sights on comedy.

I arrived in LA proudly, in my nonbinary identity, using they/them pronouns. I could no longer be an It Boy, and It Girl was still out of the question, but a silly, animal-loving, femme "IT" felt like enough for me. I was ready to get back onstage, but the theater was still shut, so stand-up comedy looked like the next best option. I started by taking classes at a lady's apartment in LA with five other students, all men. When I got up in front of them, I was surprised to find that my squeaky-clean musical theater persona left me and my inner Chelsea Handler came out. My humor turned toward the really raunchy. Here I was moving through my creative life like a Charlotte, but in reality, I was a Samantha. My comedy sets, which I would script ahead of time and memorize word for word, were stories about my past sexual experiences (and the occasional update on the opossum that I was raising in my West Hollywood kitchen). My teacher would always harp on me for being dirty, but I was so enjoying the contrast of who I was onstage before. Comedy gave me more control over my narrative, and I loved it.

I think everyone on earth should try stand-up at least once. Nothing will scare you ever again. But here's the thing about stand-up—rarely does a comic get a return on their investment. Especially in Los Angeles, where you have to drive, sit through traffic, find parking, pay for parking, pay the open mic host, only to tell jokes for five minutes to people who aren't really that interested in what you say before needing to get back in your car again. I started getting comfortable trying out my stand-up material on TikTok in casual vlog-style videos. The draw of the digital audience, plus the ease of telling jokes from my canopy bed, began to surpass the inconvenience of telling jokes on an IRL stage. And, well, that's how we got here. Once *Days of Girlhood* unexpectedly turned into a daily series, I tucked away my onstage dreams for a future date, which happened one year later, on Day 365. After that first year, I was sitting pretty thanks to all the time and effort I'd poured into TikTok. When I came out as trans, I had no intentions of being *famous* famous. That was never part of what I saw for myself, yet when I told the world who I really was, the IT factor clicked in. My following helped me get into rooms I never thought possible, like being the first trans girl to audition for certain leading-lady roles on Broadway. I kept seeing these moments where I felt like I could defy the odds. Sure, the theater world didn't really know what to do with me, but they were willing to meet me, to crack open the door and hear what I had to offer.

* * * * *

This is how I realized that TikTok created a new breed of IT Girl syndrome. Before, IT Girls were developed over time. They'd star in a movie, it'd take two years to come out, and they'd have those years to prepare. TikTok does things at an unprecedented pace. I grew a million followers in under a month. It was so contradictory to a theater trajectory. I think a major factor of my success was that I blossomed at the start of pop culture's obsession with hyperfemininity. Bimbofication. *Barbie.* I began *Days of Girlhood* during the start of a larger celebration about what womanhood could look like. A lot of us were on the internet unpacking shame, and during the unpacking of that shame I got a lot of messages from people who didn't enjoy their girlhood but said they were enjoying mine.

But being an IT Girl is a temporary title. You don't hear "IT Woman" being thrown around. I was looking to cis It Girls to compare myself to, like Emma Chamberlain or Alix Earle, but most, if not all, were leagues cooler than me, by conventional "cool" standards anyway. Not to mention, I'm trans. While I have an extreme amount of privilege, I will always be inherently controversial, and political, no matter how many brand deals or magazine covers I grace. Being a trans IT Girl means something very different. With the help of TikTok, commodification of identity, and unchecked capitalism, I unintentionally made transitioning aspirational. This, I believe, was difficult for the trans community to watch. At times, I was split in half, trying to stay grounded and earnest on one side, and trying to fully step into my X factor on the other. Showing up for the community but being selfish enough to chase my desires. So often, I would wonder what that *Grinch* theater kid version of me would think about all of the attention. Maybe they'd be slightly enamored but would probably think I was cooler when I was focusing on Broadway musicals instead of followers.

These days, sometimes I don't know if feeling like you are "the moment" is worth it. It's a dangerous thing to believe, that you have IT, that you've obtained IT, because then at any moment IT can be gone. IT is disposable. Because when IT is gone, then what's left? When kids tell me they want to grow up to be an influencer, I suppress my urge to tell them to "RUN!" Instead, I tell them to get really good at something else first, whether that's theater or music or writing or fashion. To take classes. To find their purpose, which will only grow more obvious the more they try new things. Because at the end of the day when I inevitably lose my IT Girl status, what will be left? I can still sing. I can still make people laugh. I know how to dance (not tap, though). I can still memorize lines and maybe someone will let me do that in the future. Even if it's just for fun. Having my talents to fall back on brings me a little bit of peace. But only a little.

During this whirlwind of fame and figures and success, I made a huge mistake: I got comfortable. I skyrocketed toward the sun, forgetting that flying too close could and absolutely would disintegrate me. For a brief second, I forgot that I wasn't like the cis IT Girls. I forgot that I was trans. I took brand deals that weren't on brand. And that's all it took for everything to come crumbling down.

DAY 12 of being a girl . . .

. . . And I bought tampons just in case someone might need one.

Context?

Yes!

Yesterday, while most of LA was at Sunday brunch, I was at a gay club in West Hollywood pounding mimosas and dancing to Kylie Minogue. Clubbing for me is a rare occasion, as I had a fake ID at age fifteen growing up, so I got most of the partying out of my system early. Now in my midtwenties, I prefer nights in with *Gilmore Girls* and cheap Trader Joe's wine. A friend was DJing at the club and I was on a high from my first week living proudly as a woman—the majority of my first week out as trans felt like it was lived for my followers, so I wanted to have a little fun for me.

It was easy to feel out and proud in my studio apartment, but insecurities crept in while in public, especially when it came time to tinkle. I don't pass as a cis woman, so the fear of someone calling me out or causing a scene in the ladies' room was a very real concern. Luckily, gay club bathrooms weren't as intimidating. I would walk into the women's restroom—which in a WeHo gay club should be called the "women's restroom . . . plus her gay friend, and her dog, and her gay's Grindr hookup, etc."—and finally feel like I belonged in there.

I've always preferred to sit to pee, even when I was little. I've been pee-shy most of my life, and I would opt for a stall over a urinal every time. Standing next to a stranger with your dick out is, and will always be, INSANE to me. How have we normalized this?! What if the stranger next to you sneezes and loses grip, and it showers over you? Or, worse, they purposefully whip it in your direction and it becomes the "Rain on Me" music video?! I digress. Now, as a woman, I would NEVER stand and pee, as that gives me dysphoria and is a dead giveaway to the gal next to me when my feet are facing the opposite direction. Plus, with my heels on, it would make for a much higher aim.

For quick pees, Lily taught me to squat over the seat so my booty doesn't touch. If I do use a seat liner, it usually gets wet from the person's pee dribble before me and next thing I know I'm doing a full deep clean of the toilet seat—not worth it. When sitting (or squatting, like right now), I try to aim my pee at the toilet's porcelain sides because I've noticed that peeing from a vagina sounds different than a penis. Vagina peeing is quieter. I'd hate for my penis peeing to be the thing that blows my cover. To this day, I am still pee-shy, and I have to do multiplication in my head, even if I'm alone.

As I'm squatting in my pink-and-green strappy stilettos that remind me of *The Fairly OddParents*, a voice slurs from the other stall.

A Bathroom Conversation

Stall Neighbor: HEYYYY . . . DO YOU HAVE A TAMPON ON YOU?

I freeze. Is she talking to me? There are only two stalls here . . . she must be talking to me. I pitch my voice up.

Me: Ummmm . . . Sorry, don't have one on me.

Why did I pitch my voice up?

Stall Neighbor: No worries! Toilet paper it is.

FUCK! Is this normal?

I had experience exchanging toiletries like lip gloss or powder with the occasional drunk girl, but am I now responsible for things that go inside the body? Do women have tampons on them at all times? Did I blow my cover? I know there isn't a *How to Girl 101* handbook, but right now I really wish there was.

Better pick up some tampons just to be safe.

So, this is how I ended up at the tampon aisle of the grocery store staring at the sea of options. Each box has the letters L, R, S ... WTF. I google the letters to find out their meaning—AHA! Sizes! I'm not sure about size for a stranger on the go, but it's the thought that counts, right? I bought a box of Tampax because those are the ones I saw most in commercials while binge-watching *Desperate Housewives*. Once I was back in the car, I made today's video, showing off my new purse accessories. *Maybe this will serve as an olive branch to those TERFs who are still trailing me in the comments. See? I AM on your team!* And ... post. Immediately, the view count began skyrocketing. One million, then two, then three ... I had never seen a video grow in views so fast. It really was the tampon heard around the world.

"This is so sweet. Thank you for thinking of us."

"I COULDA USED THIS LAST WEEK WHEN I DIDN'T HAVE ONE OMG"

"Instant follow!"

The olive branch worked! Victory! Wait . . . what's that?

"What a crock of shit."

"This is gross. Stay out of our restrooms and away from our kids."

"You are the reason there's a tampon shortage in this country."

How did I go from being a helpful gal pal to causing a national tampon shortage?!

Funny how something with such pure intentions can be turned into something controversial so quickly. It felt like the second I came out, I became public enemy number one. I wonder if other trans people feel this way.

Step away from the comments. Dyl, you need to remember that you know yourself and your heart better than anyone on the internet does. Your intentions are good. Please don't harden or become jaded. I think you'll be okay. Proud of you. Just keep going. Period. Ha.

LOVE YA,

Dylan

DAY 17 of being a girl . . .

. . . And I'm the bearded lady. I've felt euphoric about many parts of my biological body like my height, my frame, and my smallish shoe size. But God really said, "We can't make her toooo comfy; let's give her the thickest beard in town." I'm the kind of gal who can shave at 9 a.m. and seconds later the five o'clock shadow is already there.

When I hit puberty, my whole body erupted with thick coarse hair, most notably on my legs. I was a teenager with chicken legs that were hardly visible behind my blanket of leg pubes. In high school I basically got second-degree burns from slathering them in Nair. What can I say? I'm sensitive . . . in all of the ways. Lily recently told me her dad used to worry about how much leg hair I had, as if it was a condition. In college, I learned to trim my body hair, which made a WORLD of difference. You could actually see my skin!

Before I turned twenty-one, I sort of liked my facial hair, only because it helped me get into bars underage. My impeccable fake ID from China couldn't do its job when I was clean-shaven. While the beard masculinized me, it also made me deeply uncomfortable, but at that time in my life partying at bars took precedence over dysphoria. Alcohol helped block out the Dark Thoughts!

Once I ditched the fake ID, I wanted to get laser hair removal, but my dermatologist said that one day I might want a beard or need it for a role. I don't think so, honey! (Shout out to the *Las Culturistas* podcast, ILY.)

Now that I'm transitioning, my beard has become unbearable. Last week, I found myself on trans Reddit for the first time, where I learned orange color corrector cancels out the blue tones of a beard shadow. I immediately bought the brightest orange color corrector and applied it under my concealer and foundation, finished with powder. Accutane kicked my acne's ass, so I wouldn't have to wear much face makeup if it weren't for this beard. I love makeup, but it's still wildly intimidating. Especially the eyes. The lower half of my face now looks orange and muddy in certain lights, but it's an A for effort.

One day, I was mindlessly scrolling Insta when I saw Khloé Kardashian posted from a laser hair removal clinic. You can't throw a rock without hitting a med spa in Los Angeles, they're everywhere. I figured laser was out of my price range, but I took a shot in the dark and sent the chain a direct message to see if we could "collab," as the kids call it. To my surprise, they offered me a few free sessions in exchange for a TikTok and Insta. If oversharing my transition can lead to paying for my desired gender-affirming care, then consider me an open book!

In the lobby of said clinic, "By the Grace of God" was stenciled on the wall, and there were framed pictures of Bible quotes . . . Uh-oh. The aesthetic was so bougie I pretended not to see. Hey, they offered me a collab! They could be Jesus-loving trans allies? Even if they weren't, this beard has got to go.

The collab only covered three areas of the body, so I chose my beard, my left butt cheek, and my right butt cheek—how rude to separate them. But I figured it'd be more convenient to do everything at once, so I paid out of pocket for the rest of the body. It hurt worse when she zapped my face, especially above the lip. The privates also were a total bitch, and I wasn't sure the nurse was even going to do that area. I felt a little shame as she directed me to "pull my shaft up and to the left! Now the right! Good job!"

I was also excited to get rid of my chest hair. It
serves as full-on '70s shag carpet if I let it grow.
One of my worst fears is growing boobs and still
having a hairy chest. I'm PRAYING the timeline
works—out with the chest hair, in with the tits.
After an hour and a half of zapping my pubes in God's
house, I was done and ready to debut my dolphin body.

A Conversation with My Laser Nurse

Nurse: You're all set! Just no shaving
for seven to ten days.

Me: Even on my face?!

Nurse: Even on your face. And don't forget
to make your next appointment.

Me: My next appointment?

Nurse: You'll need at least eight sessions,
if not more, to clear an area.

I look down at all the areas that would need clearing.
For a brief moment, I'm distracted by the midsize
loan I'd need to complete the task, to then realize
I have to live with a full beard for a week out of
every month going forward until it's gone for good.
My glass-half-full mentality kicks in: I could
wear a mask for certain outings, but what about my
Days of Girlhood videos? Isn't the whole point to
celebrate and show off my newfound femininity?

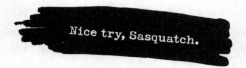
Nice try, Sasquatch.

I decided at the beginning of this journey that I'd show the good, the bad, and the ugly. This, my friend, is my ugly. At least it is to me.

Staying inside for the past week wasn't as difficult as I had thought, since I don't have a real job and I'm happy to hide in my canopy bed for long periods of time. Tonight, I started to get canopy bed fever and said screw it, let's go see a play. But before I went out to face the real world, I decided to show my followers my biggest insecurity: my lady beard. And after six days, it ain't just stubble, it's braidable. I filmed the video in my bathroom mirror, so they could see things from my perspective. I posted and then went out to see *Buyer & Cellar* on a Me date.

When I got home, I checked the beard video to find it blowing up . . . and for encouraging reasons this time:

"I'm a cis woman and I shave every day!"

"Thank you for sharing this with us. You still look beautiful."

"Lady beards unite!!!!"

I am OVER THE MOON happy I shared my beard with the world. Wanna know why? Because now it doesn't have power over me. I made it my bitch. It also allows me to be a lot more casual in looks going forward. I never want to get to a place where I need to be all done up in full glam in order to be perceived. I think a lot of trans femmes feel the pressure to be as passing as possible 24/7, and today I found comfort in accepting my body for where she is at this moment. And don't confuse this peace to be euphoria; I'm still gonna go World War III on this beard, but while she is here, I won't hate her.

Speaking of hate, a lot of the nasty comments I've gotten point out my beard. "I can see your five o'clock shadow." NO SHIT, SHERLOCK! Do people think we trans folks are that delusional?! We SEE those physical traits magnified by a thousand in comparison to what cis people see us as. It is at times a debilitating level of self-awareness. But to let those things hold us back from coming out, or making content, or entering society would be such a disappointment, since we trans folks have so much goodness to share. Always have and always will.

In the meantime, if Ryan Murphy decides to do a reboot of *American Horror Story: Freak Show* and Kathy Bates is unavail to play the bearded lady, I'm his gal.

LOVE YA,

Dylan

DAY 30 of being a girl . . .

. . . And I'm attending my first red carpet tonight!
Sort of. The first one I was *personally* invited to.
Technically, Alyah's premiere for *The Sex Lives of
College Girls* six months ago was my first red carpet.
When Alyah invited me, I was so excited to attend a
real Hollywood event. I hit up my favorite chunky
knit designer, Hope Macaulay, who sent me a colorful
custom dress. I was quickly ego-checked when I tried
to step onto the carpet, just to find out not everyone invited gets to walk the physical carpet. I always
imagined the carpet led straight up to the door, but,
disappointingly, it's in a side room that feels . . .
less glamorous. I sheepishly walked up to the women
with clipboards, explaining to the publicist ladies
that the dress designer expected red carpet photos,
and they took pity on me. This was my first lesson on
the power of kindness in Hollywood and how humility
can go a long way. I got to proudly walk next to Alyah
and got some of my favorite Instas ever. Thank you,
publicist ladies!

But tonight, I got an invite addressed to ME! It was for
the Fashion LA Awards, which I hadn't heard of, but you
bet your ass that I'm gonna say yes to free drinks and
a chance to get a good Insta post.

To prepare for the festivities, I worked with my first
stylist ever this week, Branden. I like Branden because
he's young and talented, and most of all because he
could work in my tight budget. Before today, I had no
idea how stylists work. From what I've gathered, the
stylist reaches out to a bunch of brands and drives
around town pitching you to different designers in
hopes that they'll dress you. You pay the stylist a
flat fee, and that includes accessories, shoes, and
fittings. Alterations and shipping are extra. You
do NOT get to keep the outfit, which is a little sad,
especially if the stylist fee is more than the cost
of the dress. But I guess that's Hollywood, baby.

Factors include:

**HOW FAMOUS
YOU ARE**

**HOW WELL-KNOWN
YOUR STYLIST IS**

HOW COOL THE EVENT IS

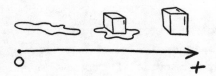

**HOW WELL YOU CAN
SERVE CUNT ON THE
RED CARPET**

(MOST IMPORTANT)

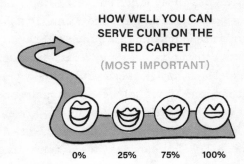

I've only been on the industry's radar for about a month now, so I was thrilled when Branden showed up to my apartment with a rack full of the cutest clothes I'd ever seen. I tried on like five winning dresses, and it was one of the most difficult decisions of my life. P.S., that's another sad part of this process—you try on so many cute things that you can't show to anyone, and then they go back to the designer to be worn by some other cuntier pair of legs. A moment of silence for the dresses that don't make the cut.

I went with an all-white cocktail dress decked out in feathers. I chose this one because it covered my chest so people wouldn't know I was flat as a board. I was a little nervous that it gave *White Chicks* swan dress vibes (my editor has since informed me that Björk did it first, but I love a niche 2000s reference, so it stays), but this dress was more tasteful. I think. I hope? My style is "borderline Halloween costume" anyway, so the look was serving. Moroccanoil, a beauty brand, offered to do my hair for the event for FREE. I can't believe someone is willing to do it for free . . .

Wait . . . have I talked about the PR gifting packages yet?

HONEY.

So, a brand DMs you with something like: "Hey girlie, we'd LOVE to send you our new *insert beauty product here* and it would be so amazing if you'd share it with your followers! XO."

These packages are wasteful and problematic . . . but my god . . . I LOVE FREE SHIT. I have done enough therapy to realize that my love of free things comes from a deep scarcity complex in which I believe I am not good enough or talented enough or pretty enough to be given anything ever. Gifts, compliments, opportunities, I always feel like anything given to me will be taken away the second people realize that I'm not as good/talented/pretty as I seem.

So, for someone to send me something in the mail, on purpose, because they enjoy me and my platform, BLOWS MY MIND. I hope I always feel this grateful. This newfound fame is a slippery slope for me; while it has helped quiet some of my inner critic thoughts, it invites millions of other critics to the party. Sometimes I worry that I'm only becoming famous for being trans. What happens when I've gotten my procedures and there are no more taboo topics to cover anymore? Part of me wants to enjoy this fame, but the other part knows that at any moment, it could burn me. As for now, I'm just gonna lead with humor and try to enjoy the ride.

Back on topic! The Fashion LA Awards—so, usually you would get your hair done at the same time as your makeup at home, but since this was a gifting service, I was instructed to go to a conference room to get my hair done first. The room was filled with other influencers

propped in front of mirrors, sipping champagne and
videoing themselves yelling over the sound of blow-
dryers. I sat down, asked for a palm tree ponytail, and
started peeking around to see what the other girls
were doing. It amazes me how much influencers don't
feel embarrassed about making content in public.
I can yap away to the camera in my canopy bed all
day long, but once I hit the streets, I freeze up.

That changes today. I mimicked the confidence of the
other influencer gals, snapping away at the different
hair products, tagging everything in sight, champagne
boomerangs, you name it. I was the only trans girl in
the room, but the other girls asked me to be in their
content, which made me feel nice. Being included by
other women is something I will never take for granted.

Then, I had to rush home to have my makeup done. A
makeup artist friend of a friend beat my face, and
babe, it rocked my world. I wish that every trans
femme human on earth could experience getting full
glam done at least once. As surface level as it may
sound, it is the most euphoric experience ever ever
ever. I put the dress on and nearly cried looking in
the mirror. I don't think I passed as a cis woman,
but it's the closest I'd ever felt to actually loving
what I saw in the reflection. No time for tears even
if they're happy ones—we can't ruin the makeup!

The event was at the Beverly Wilshire, aka the hotel
from *Pretty Woman*. I showed up on the early side,

because I knew that I'd have a better shot of getting on the carpet if I got there before the big celebs arrived. This time, the clipboard ladies ushered me onto the carpet announcing my name to the photographers, who, to my surprise, actually took photos.

I had no idea how to hold myself or pose, but I smiled as much as possible. I don't understand why some celebs take themselves so seriously and only Zoolander on the red carpet. We look good, there are gift bags, we're at an event, this should be fun?!

I survived the chaos of the carpet and started to make my way around the room where the ceremony was being held. I didn't get a plus-one, which didn't bother me at all because I love hanging out with myself. It's also a great way to network and meet new people because you aren't tethered to someone else. I popped around to the brand booths because . . . repeat after me . . . *WE! LOVE! FREE! SHIT!!!*

I felt a tap on my shoulder as I stood in line at the bar and turned around to see the most beautiful blonde woman I'd ever seen in real life, then my brain caught up with my eyes and I realized it was Gigi Gorgeous. Oh my god. Gigi Gorgeous is standing in front of me. Gigi is an OG internet icon, documenting her trans journey on YouTube not dissimilar to mine on TikTok. I loved her vlogging style, and her videos were helpful on more than one occasion.

A Conversation with Trans Icon Gigi Gorgeous

Gigi: Hey, girl.

Me: Gigi?! Oh my god. I love your YouTube videos!

Gigi: Then follow me back on TikTok!

My jaw dropped. I had zero idea she followed me, and I can't believe I had the audacity to not follow her back.

Gigi's Husband, Nats: We watch your videos every night in bed . . .

Me: I just watched your video on electrolysis.
I think I may go that route too.

Gigi: Your hair is super dark. Laser should do the trick. I couldn't go that route since I'm blonde.

We exchanged numbers, and I was over-the-moon thrilled by the new friendship. I didn't have any trans gal friends other than a few mutuals on the internet.

The award show itself was to honor different stylists and glam teams in the industry, and their celeb clients showed up to support. I had my first Kardashian spotting: Kris and Kendall were presenting an award. Along with Joe Biden and Lady Gaga, the Kardashians are on a short list of people who I'd previously thought actually were fictional characters, so seeing them IRL was pretty surreal.

As transfixed as I was during the ceremony, all those free beverages caught up with me, so to the ladies' room I went, and let me tell you, everyone and their mother was in the women's bathroom during the awards show. I even saw Megan Fox fixing her makeup in the mirror. (There was nothing to fix, she looked absolutely perfect.) Meanwhile, my five o'clock shadow was starting to say hello. I walked outside for some air and saw a blonde woman waiting by the valet . . .

KATHY HILTON!

I've watched enough *Real Housewives of Beverly Hills* to know that Kathy made the show ten thousand times more hilarious. I figured I'd introduce myself.

A Conversation with Kathy Hilton

Me: Hi, Kathy, I'm Dylan. Love you so much on *Beverly Hills*.

Kathy: I know you!

Me: You do?

Kathy: I've seen you walk in New York Fashion Week.

She had the wrong brunette.

Me: Uh, I don't think so. I've never done that. I'm trans.

Kathy: Now wait a minute . . . YOU'RE TRANS?!

Me: Yes?

Kathy: I woulda bet a million dollars you were born a girl. God, you're stunning, sweetie.

I took this as the best compliment I'd ever received. KATHY HILTON THINKS I'M PASSING!!! As Kathy's car pulled up, I used some of my newfound influencer confidence to ask her something I'd never asked anyone before: "Would you be willing to be in my TikTok? You just have to say, 'Day 30 of being a girl.'" She did it! Her publicist walked up as the car doors opened for her, and she asked me, "What's your name again?"

I responded, "Dylan Mulvaney."

"You should go by Dilly."

"Get Dilly's number," Kathy told her publicist. "I want to have her over sometime. She's a hoot."

I gave him my number, waved them off, and trotted back to my seat as the ceremony was ending. Once the lights came up, I looked around and realized I was one of the last people there, as others hovered in the lobby to find out where the afterparty was. I didn't need one of those, I had enough fun tonight to last me for weeks. If I were still my college self, I would've

overstayed my welcome, but these days I know how
to leave on a high note before things get messy.

When I got home, I dreaded washing off the makeup.
I didn't want to come back to reality just yet. But my
beard was now the length of basmati rice, so I decided
I'd take off the foundation but leave on the eye shadow
to see if I could salvage it for the next day. My palm
tree was starting to wilt, and taking out that snatched
pony was a huge relief. I climbed into my canopy
bed, ordered Domino's, and a text lit up my screen.

Kathy loved meeting you.
We'll be in touch for a time you can come over to visit.

In the words of Annie the orphan, "I THINK I'M GONNA
LIKE IT HERE!"

LOVE YA,

Dylan

Chapter 2

BEERGATE

I hate it here. Earth, that is. The Dark Thoughts that had been dissipating over the last year were rushing back in like a tsunami. After another disheartening phone call with my team that ended in tears, all I craved was a cigarette. Minutes before, I paced naked around my kitchen, tears welling in my eyes, yelling into the speakerphone, "I DON'T CARE IF I NEVER MAKE ANOTHER FUCKING DOLLAR EVER AGAIN, I JUST WANT TO DO THE RIGHT THING!!!" I can't wait to see Dakota Fanning put her spin on that line when she inevitably is cast as me in a biopic. As upsetting as the phone call was, I cracked an unexpected smile—I had never raised my voice to my team like that before. Nice to know I had a little fight left in me. I deserved a cigarette. I didn't even know if the general store at the bottom of the hill sold them, but I drove down to check. They did.

I bought. Back home. Robe on. Sad girl check.

We're going to refer to the happenings in which I partnered with a major beer company in 2023 as Beergate. Usually when we add the "-gate" suffix, it infers that some bad shit went down, and girl . . . this was baaaaad. Honestly, if you drink, this would be an EXCELLENT moment to grab a beer before continuing. Nothing would make me happier. As a matter of fact, I'll do the same. [*Walks to fridge and back, cracking open an undisclosed, non-transphobic beer brand.*] Ah, okay, let's do this.

I love me an alcoholic beverage. My dad got sober when I was three, so I knew alcoholism ran in my family. I've had my fair share of drunken nights, but never to a point where I thought I had a problem.

I typically only drink socially and am very particular when picking my poison. I love red wine, never white (also makes me projectile), but somehow champagne is okay? Maybe it's the bubbles. I never do shots. I haven't in years. As I've gotten more publicly known, people always try to buy me shots, but I always hand them off. I love an espresso martini, but only decaf, I can't do caffeine. Also, I'm allergic to tequila. I don't have a clinical diagnosis, but every time a drop touches my lips, I projectile vomit, so that seems like enough evidence to hold up in court. Sometimes I'll still indulge if I'm on a beach in Mexico and I quietly wade into the water to burp up acid. Woof. I'll do vodka quarterly, usually a Moscow mule or dirty Shirley Temple if I feel slutty. But there is nothing I prefer more than an ice-cold beer.

Reasons beer sparks trans joy for me:

1. It seems so contradictory to my overall aesthetic, and I love to surprise people
2. Its carbs fill me and Tammy the Tapeworm up, so we are full
3. It doesn't get me too drunk, so I still have my wits about me
4. I'm Irish!!!

When my agents asked me what my dream brands were, I always said Tiffany's and beer. Any beer really. I am soooo not picky. I drank Pabst Blue Ribbon in college and still would! When I found out that tagging brands on Instagram stories was a good way to get their attention, I went ham for the beer brands. I'd snap photos of myself with a Corona, or a Modelo, and tag 'em. I went to a Dodgers game (also off brand for me) and got a tall can of Generic Beer. Snap! Tag. Post.

* * * * *

One January morning, I opened my email to see what my agent had for me that day. At the top of my inbox was a shiny subject line that read, "Offer: Generic Beer." I couldn't believe my beer dreams were coming true! My agent said, "No need to decide right away, we're also speaking with Other Beer Company* and we want them to battle over you!" A beer battle?! Over little old ME?!! HEAVEN!! After a few pay increases from both, the other brand finally backed down and Generic Beer took me as their prizewinning trans girl. I sometimes wonder had I gone with that other company if any of the following would have transpired, but no point in living in what-ifs, right? My first Generic Beer social media ad dropped on February 11, 2023. TikTok doesn't allow for alcohol advertisements, so this was strictly an Instagram deal. A few transphobic rumblings in the comments under this first video, but nothing out of the ordinary. While staying at the Plaza in New York, Generic Beer sent me a can with my face on it. I had gotten a lot of PR sent to me over the past year, but this was by far my favorite thing I'd received. My dad was particularly obsessed with it, as if this can was what solidified my fame in his eyes. I packed it away until the next time they reached out to make a video ad surrounding March Madness.

"March Madness" resonated with me—not because of sports, but because of Day 365 and everything happening during that month. My career was on the upswing, now expanding from social media campaigns to speaking engagements, major auditions, and public appearances. I spent March bopping from New York to LA to Pittsburgh to New Orleans to Copenhagen and back to New York. I brought the custom can with me to New Orleans, where Bryn and Frankie (my IT Girl and IT Boy college role models) were getting married. I filmed the Generic Beer video in my hotel room before the wedding, in full Audrey Hepburn glam, playing up my aloofness to sports, which is very, very real. The video was approved, and I posted it when arriving in New York, on April 1.

---

* Girl, you know I *wish* I could tell you, but my lawyer would burn me at the stake. Love you, Reggie!

"This better be an April Fools' prank," someone comments on my video. A few more negative comments than usual. Huh. Must have gotten shared somewhere lame. I went about my Monday, which included singing in MCC's *Miscast* cabaret alongside Josh Groban, Ben Platt, and Rachel Zegler. This was the kind of gig that would've made little Dylan giddy. I performed "Man Up" from *The Book of Mormon*, complete with a tear-away dress moment. After the gala, a casting director came up to me and said, "I don't know how you handle all the hate. You're so strong." I brushed it off with an "Oh, it's nothing I can't handle!" LOL. Bet?

"I don't understand why they can't just condemn violence. How difficult is it to say, 'Hey we don't hate trans people and you shouldn't take to automatic weapons in order to show your loathing of them.'" I'm on the phone forty-eight hours later with my publicist and agent, after Kid Rock posted a video of shooting beer cans with a rifle. I remember sitting in the Plaza lobby for this call, partly in shock over his response, partly peeved that this was throwing a wrench in my busy week. I didn't feel all that anxious over it, thinking that I still had the brand's support and they would do the right thing. "We're trying to connect them with GLAAD to have a meeting on how to fix this," my publicist replied, soothing my anxieties. I had hoped that this could be a positive step in the right direction. Maybe Generic Beer will take a stand against hate and Middle America will come around to trans people and it will all be for the better.

I headed back to LA, and by the time I landed, my advertisement was the top headline for every conservative news source. I started to feel a weight pressing on my chest, knowing that this was some of the worst levels of transphobia I'd ever received, especially from proper media and not just dumbass podcast hosts. I called my life coach, Mory, who I'd like to trademark as the Queer Celebrity Whisperer. Mory said matter-of-factly, "Baby, get ready. You just got a lot more famous." I challenged her, "But not in a good way?!" She reassured me, "You were meant for this, and you can absolutely handle it." She was right, I've made it this far, haven't I? Thank GOD I'd been working with Mory before all this went down. Imagine me trying to unpack all this with a brand-new therapist, like, "Heyyyyyy. So . . . I might have incited a little culture war, but let's talk about my childhood ;)."

While dropping off packages to UPS, I went to get back in my car and a man ran up to me with a camera and asked, "Dylan, what do you have to say to Kid Rock?!"

My fight or flight kicked in, and I struggled to find my keys. I looked like a deer in the headlights and felt genuinely scared. I finally got in my car, and he put the camera down. "Hey, I'm not going to hurt you, but you should get used to this. We're not the bad guys." I drove away from my first paparazzo, adrenaline pumping, and called my team to ask about security. I'd never felt like I needed any personal protection up until this point. Sometimes the organizers of events will offer personal security as a general precaution. I notoriously drove my bodyguards crazy because I would squeeze past them to greet and hug anyone and everyone who approached me. Being followed by a random man with a camera made the impact of Kid Rock's video finally feel real. While I wasn't scared of Kid Rock himself showing up to my house to fuck me up, I was afraid one of his fans might find me and do something stupid.

Back at home, I was a little spooked. Is being followed my new reality? I googled "Dylan Mulvaney paparazzi" and was shocked to find photos of me taking in my trash cans just the day before. There I am, post–laser hair removal with not a care in the world. I looked rough in the photos, but at least my goose purse added some camp. Who took those photos? I peeked out my front window to see two cars out front, ones I'd never seen before. I went out my gate to investigate, and BOOM: camera lens. I hit the deck on my hands and knees. *How'd they get my address? Who cares enough to wait outside for hours just to snap me? If the quote-un-quote Good Guys can find me, can the Bad Guys find me too?*

Lily came over to stay with me, and she is both the best and the worst plus-one in moments of disaster, because although I feel peace when I'm near her, she also spirals to the worst possible conclusions. "What if someone breaks in here while we're sleeping and kills me too?!" she half jokes, half seriously asks. "Don't worry, you're blonde and they'll go for the brunette first." Our spirals were slightly calmed by the bodyguard who was now positioned in my driveway. Generic Beer wouldn't agree to pay for security, but the third-party brand agency that hired me had agreed, and thank God, because I have money, but not bodyguard money. Our guard was smaller than both Lily and me, but he had a gun. Fighting fire with fire.

For weeks, I went stir-crazy inside my house, not wanting to give the paparazzi outside anything to work with. "Honey, I want you to hire full glam, strut out to the mailbox in some kitten heels, and give those photographers a run for their money," said Jonathan Van Ness on one of our frequent FaceTime calls. I'd immediately fallen in love with JVN after bingeing *Queer Eye* in college, and now to have them as a real-life BFF brought me immense joy. But even JVN's sassy and heartwarming attitude couldn't distract me from the anxiety and adrenaline of being the conservative news punching bag of the moment. I was fixated on fixing this mess.

Initially, I had hoped this ad would be a positive step toward trans acceptance. That hope was now gone. After feeling disappointed by the statements released by Generic Beer brand, where I personally felt they did not condemn hate toward the trans community, I no longer waited for their support. I was gonna have to fix this on my own, and I immediately thought to do what I do best: make a video and talk to my followers. The connection and honesty with my audience was the only thing keeping me going. I needed them to know that I was hurting, the community was hurting, and that they shouldn't support transphobic corporations. But one little thing stood in the way: my contract.

I've learned a LOT this year about corporate law, something I never thought I'd need unless I was cast in a *Legally Blonde* reboot. If I learned anything, it's that large sums of money and contracts don't generally pair well with empathy and doing the right thing. I listened to my lawyer, and agents, and publicists and managers, all urging me to let this die down quietly. But their advice had me in a stalemate because . . . it wasn't dying down. Somehow, even a month later, news stations were still reporting on the ad every single day. Memes of me continued going viral. Boycotts were sticking. I stayed quiet and felt all of the self-love, confidence, and strength I had found this last year leave my body with every passing day.

The corporate marketing system I had briefly been accepted into, despite my trans identity, was now reminding me just how much it hated trans people. No amount of palatability or privilege could save me. TikTok fattened me up. Big corporate bought me. And the media devoured me.

I was the sacrificial lamb these beer drinkers needed in order to push their transphobic rhetoric across the finish line. My dream of transcending social media fame to make it into mainstream media finally came true, but not for the right reasons. My blips of social media prestige had provided brief moments of warmth, but the persistent spotlight was burning me from the outside in.

I almost felt like I was being canceled, but I knew I didn't fit the typical cancellation category. I ran through the Ten Commandments from my childhood in Catholic school. Unless there's an eleventh that's Thou Shalt Not Promote Beer Whilst Transitioning, I hadn't broken any of them. Little Dylan couldn't figure out what she did wrong, and adult Dylan didn't have the answers. All she had was a blossoming nicotine addiction. The truth is, I was being canceled by bigots, who never greenlit me to begin with. Up until this point, these transphobes felt like fictional characters operating on the outskirts of my world, rarely to be acknowledged from my bubble. But now, with the obvious sheer numbers of those against me, I started to question the humans that exist inside my safe spaces.

I became paranoid. I wondered if the people who loved me, some for my entire life, secretly felt ashamed of their association with me. Did they see me as a woman? Could my mailman be a Judas? Was my smiling Trader Joe's cashier one of the haters in my comments?

My paranoia wasn't completely unwarranted because, during this time, I had knowledge that someone in my inner circle was potentially sharing my personal details with the press. Even though I didn't know who, exactly, it was, I have never experienced a deeper heartbreak than when I had to question the solidarity of my most trusted companions. I called my dad to fill him in on this situation, knowing deeply that it wasn't him, and started to cry.

I heard him start to get choked up too. A minute went by without words.

"Maybe your life is different now, and we just have to get used to that," he reasoned, both of us unsure if he meant this as a positive or a negative. Whichever the case, it hit us hard.

"Yeah, maybe," I responded.

"You know what they say in my AA, right?"

I already knew, but I let him say it anyway.

"God grant me the serenity to accept the things I cannot change, the courage to change the things I can, and the wisdom to know the difference."

In all the years my dad had been repeating this prayer, it was the first time it felt like it actually applied to me. The problem was, it's not in my nature to accept the things I cannot change. I immediately try and fix. But there was no fixing this. So, I had to hope for the wisdom to know the difference.

DAY 42 of being a girl . . .

. . . And am I . . . STRAIGHT?! I was scrolling my TikTok comments today and someone wrote, "God, Dylan is cute . . . too bad she's straight." STRAIGHT?! There's no way. The math isn't mathing. I had been labeled gay before I could even walk; there was something faggy about the way I crawled as a toddler—Wait, if I'm straight now, can I not say "faggy"?! FUCK!!!!

                    Breathe. Pause for a second.

Let's take stock of my greatest hits. (P.S. The names have been changed for my own personal entertainment.)

Boy Scout Billy
Him: 18, Me: 14

My first boyfriend (if you could even call him that). My mom read our texts while I was in the shower and had a full-on breakdown. She confiscated my phone and demanded I end the two-week-long relationship. So, I "did" but continued to secretly call him on my hamburger phone landline. It was all so exciting

and felt very *Romeo and Juliet*.
Once she gave me my phone back,
I lost interest and broke up with
him. I was savage even then.
P.S. I now see the age gap was
problematic, but in his defense, he
was still a Boy Scout at the time.

Sloppy Seconds Steven
Him: 24, Me: 18

Sloppy Seconds Steven lived on my
street, and Lily dated him for a
summer. As soon as she left for a
semester abroad, I stepped in for
the role of Occasional Jacuzzi
Hook Up. Sloppy Seconds Steven
was definitely in cahoots with the
drug cartel. After his drunken
oversharing, he tried to get
me to sign an NDA, but I knew
even back then that it would
be a good story for a book. And,
don't worry, Lily loves that we
hooked up with the same guy.

Irish Prince Patrick
Him: 27, Me: 21

On a solo trip to Europe,
after seeing *Riverdance* in
Dublin and indulging in some
Guinness, I found myself
alone at a gay bar where I met
a potential love of my life,
Patty. We spent five glorious
days together until finally
having earth-shattering
sex. On the last night, I
discovered that his family
had royal ties. Sure, Ireland
no longer has royals, and this
relationship lasted a week,
but it reawakened my delusion
of becoming a princess.

Verdict: All of my past flings
are cisgender he/hims . . .
which now, being a woman,
makes me . . . straight?

I loved being gay. While it created a decent amount of
shame in my early years, I finally got to a place where
I celebrated my gayness. My sexuality became an
escape where I could mask my femininity as twink
behavior:

- When I purchased women's clothes, I blamed it on my gayness.

- When I wore makeup, I chalked it up to being gay.

- When I slept with men in order to feel something? GAY!!!

Riiightttt? Wrong, Miss Mulvaney.

Those were manifestations of my transness poking through a very dense fabric of shame.

Not to say gay men doing those things makes them trans, but for me it was easier to label myself as a flamboyant gay boy than to face the reality of my impending gender journey. So, it makes sense why I'd be apprehensive to leave behind the Gay label. Let's see where I'm at now:

Despite me not understanding them at all, I'm still attracted to cis men. I'm intimidated by sleeping with women, but I'm definitely open. I like the idea of being with a trans man because we could connect over identity. Gender nonconformity is hot to me. Hell, I still live off the binary in some ways. Shout out to the "she/THEY" in my bio. If you plug all of this into one of those *Cosmo* quizzes in the back of the magazine titled "What sexuality are you?" I think it might result in: girlie, you are *Queer*! *Gasp* QUEER! I LIKE THE TERM "QUEER"!

Funny how that word was so vulgar just a few years ago. Growing up, the kids in my mom's apartment complex would play "Smear the Queer." All I remember is balls being thrown at my face and being tackled continuously . . . and not in the fun way. Surprise, I was the queer!

Queer feels like I can explore my sexuality without being constrained to the toxic ideas that gay men subscribe to when they talk about vaginas.

I haven't had much airtime with a vagina since I left my mom's. I do have an epic photo of me in the delivery room, still halfway in, flashing a peace sign while I entered this wild world. I would include that photo, but I think I've put my mom through enough grief already.

Twenty-one years to the day, I had my next run-in with a vagina. I was in Vegas for my twenty-first birthday with Lily and my two gay friends, and Lily offered to give us gays an anatomy lesson when we got home from the club. She spread-eagle on the bed, and we all let out:

Ooo!

Ahhh!

Whoa!

At that moment, I realized the vagina wasn't something to fear; in fact, I found it quite attractive. I don't think penises are particularly cute, and what I was seeing was way more approachable.

All this sexy talk is making me realize, I haven't slept with someone in three and a half years. I'm nervous for that first hookup as a girl—no matter who I jump into bed with. Part of me would be more comfortable being with a penis, since I've been to that rodeo before, but now that I'm a different gender entirely, shaking things up could be good for this backwards cowgirl.

I haven't been kissed as a girl. That needs to change ASAP. But I have an opportunity to do it right this time. I don't need to compromise my values or my body in the way I did as a gay man. Be patient. Your prince (or princess) is coming.

LOVE YA,

Dylan ♥

DAY 73 of being a girl . . .

. . . And I am someone's daughter. My dad called me today. I could hear the excitement in his voice as he went into his story.

A Conversation with My Dad

Dad: Dyl, you'll never believe it.

Me: What?

Dad: I'm on this tiny little island off Bora Bora and there's four people here total. I introduced myself to them as Jim Mulvaney, and this random French woman goes, "Are you related to Dylan Mulvaney?" I say, "Yes, that's my son!" She got stern and said, "No, that's your daughter. I've been following her journey online, and she is amazing."

Me: Wow! What a small world. Tell her "Hey" for me.

Dad: I am really, really proud to call you my daughter. I hope you know that.

I got choked up, but I tend to mask my emotions with my dad since we aren't overly gushy with each other.

Me: Aw, thank you, Dad, that means a lot.

Dad: Love you.

Me: Love you too!

In reality, it meant the world. To hear my conservative, Catholic, football-loving, mismatched-sock-wearing father call me his daughter was the gift I'd waited to hear for so much of my life. It was also hard not to feel embarrassed, because I always feared it was too difficult or a nuisance to make the shift for him. "He" to "she" feels doable—son to daughter feels like a big ask. But he answered.

I hung up the phone and decided to make today's TikTok surrounding this convo. I probably should've asked him if I could, but I was too excited. This is a real, tangible change. My dad has formed a relationship with my new identity and is seeing me for who I am. Not a monster, but his child. If my dad, who is

the number one creature of habit, can change, I have a lot of hope for the rest of this world too. And big shout-out to that French lady who talked with him.

When my mom was pregnant with me, my dad would sweep the bases at the Little League stadium as a way to solidify his spot as coach when I was old enough to play baseball. I didn't quite fulfill that desire, seeing that I wanted absolutely nothing to do with sports and everything to do with dance. It was very *Billy Elliot* (gen z, google it). Jim was really chill with letting go of some of those expectations, probably because I was unexpected myself. Before I was born, my dad believed he was infertile until he surprisingly got my mom pregnant. Now, I'm his only child. Although we couldn't be more different in many ways, I think he's just happy to have me no matter who I am.

Jim never quite figured out my they/them pronouns last year, so when I came out as a woman, that made more sense to him than the concept of nonbinary. When anyone misgenders me, I tend to be very understanding, especially with my family and people who have known me for a long time. I am in constant conflict with myself when it comes to my relationship with family. I feel guilty that I am complicating their cookie-cutter lives and that I create a burden where there was none before. They still want a connection with me, shouldn't that be a major win? When I do engage, it comes with misgendering. Sometimes I don't have the energy to put up with the misgendering, but they feel that "I need to be around more often so that they can try to get the pronouns right."

Jim shows love in the way he knows how: buying things from Costco (even if you don't need them). This is my dad's form of care currency. He once bought me high-end ski goggles during the summer, when I hadn't skied in ten years, "just in case."

Unfortunately for Jim, there is nothing at Costco that could help him understand more about my gender journey. My dad's generation didn't talk about feelings but showed love through something tangible. I'm the opposite; I could talk and cry and hug and overshare all day long. Today was a turning point for us both. Now if only I could get him to stop calling me every time he meets a gay person to see if I know them, that would be the greatest win of all.

LOVE YA,

Dylan ♥

DAY 89 of being a girl . . .

. . . And today I learned how to tuck.

TUCK /tək/ a technique whereby an individual hides the crotch bulge of the penis and testicles so that they are not conspicuous through clothing.

I still wear Calvin Klein men's underwear because I didn't think women's panties could accommodate my "situation." I usually refrain from clothing that hugs that area so that it doesn't draw attention, but last week I bought a pair of little pleather shorts from Aritzia that didn't feel too crotch-tastic. I took them for a spin at the Grove in LA (my Disneyland, remember?), but it felt less and less like the happiest place on earth when I started getting stares at my camel toe from tourists. Why were people so obsessed with what I had going on down there? By strangers' looks you'd think I was wearing a G-string in public. To deal with my discomfort, I came up with a silly song titled "Normalize the Bulge." I decided to make it a video because maybe someone else online could relate, whether cis or trans.

What came next was a wave of disapproving messages from certain trans women shaming me for not tucking. I don't have a specific shame attached to acknowledging my privates at this moment in time: I am a woman with a penis.

What I'm gathering is that some trans folks believe passing, or at least attempting to pass, should be common courtesy for the cis people existing with us in society. Passing as a biological woman wasn't the original goal of my transition, but passing is something that is being taught to me over time. I am known quite publicly as a trans person, so no matter how hard I try to pass, I may never have the ability to blend into the sea of cis. In some ways, I'd prefer not to pass . . . like what if I was at a bar and a cute guy walked up to me and didn't know I was trans? I think the comfort in not passing right now is that the people interacting with me are well aware of my identity and choose to associate with me anyway.

I feel so far away from passing that I don't know if that's a healthy mindset for me to commit to, as I might spend the next chapter of my life yearning for something that may never come. I was comfortable living openly as a trans woman, but I lacked the life experience of the women in my comments. Those trans women's concerns surrounding my bulge started to feel more warranted; maybe they were trying to keep me and other trans women safe because they knew the dangers of not passing.

In my pursuit of not giving trans people a bad rep, I ordered some tucking tape that looked easy enough to operate. Tucking tape is sort of like a giant Band-Aid that starts below your belly button and flosses up between your cheeks to your lower back. It took a few tries to see a slight result. Maybe I'm packing heat or doing it wrong because I was left with a sizable, fleshy nothingness where my privates once were, which I can only describe as a Barbie pouch. (Ooo girl, "Barbie pouch" will upset conservatives, but this one feels worth it—into the book it goes!)

I wore the tucking tape to an event with a pretty tight dress, and it made peeing HELLISH. I brought two pieces of tape in my purse as backups because they aren't reusable, but it was still a nightmare. Cue infomercial lady: There's gotta be a better way!

ISADORA ENTERS CHAT

Isadora is a trans gal I follow on Instagram who reached out to me at the beginning of my *Days of Girlhood* journey. I didn't have a ton of trans friends, and she really made an effort to support me, standing up for me in my comments and checking in frequently. She's visiting LA right now and kept inviting me to her hotel, so tonight, I'm joining her for happy hour. When I arrive, she is barside with another trans girlie, Tracey. We all have Aperols and I get grilled:

"What doctor does your hormones?"

"What's your estrogen dosage?"

"Do you want a pussy?"

"I could see you with a full B."

These are perfect examples of what NOT to say when you're a cis person meeting a trans human, but this is what the dolls refer to as "Trans Table Talk." Doll friendships can be varied and our interests and hobbies have little to do with our identity, but when we trans gals get together, it can be fun to compare and contrast our experiences. I'm sure there are many trans women who are not as forthcoming with personal info even among other dolls, but I'm such an open book, and these women made me feel safe.

After Trans Table Talk, I shifted the convo to something more neutral.

A Conversation with Isadora and Tracey

Me: What are you doing in LA?

Isadora: I'm working.

Me: Oooh, what kind of work?

Isadora: Sex work.

Tracey: I do it too!

Isadora: I needed money for my surgeries fast. Girl, we don't all have brand deal money coming in like you.

She didn't sound judgmental at all, but it still made me sit with my privilege for a moment. I could count on two hands the number of trans women on TikTok that I had seen doing paid partnerships. Some of these companies hadn't hired a trans person before me. Instead of my body, I capitalize off my vulnerability. You can say a lot about trans people, but we know how to find creative ways to keep the lights on and the doctors' visits paid for. A girl's gotta do what a girl's gotta do.

"You're like the trans Ellen! Very palatable. It's important," Isadora says. Growing up, Ellen was one of my greatest role models—she made gay people seem not only normal but fun and relatable. When I started building an audience, I tried really hard to clean up my act so that people wouldn't judge me for being trans. I love cursing and talking about sex, and I've done drugs, but I thought those things would hurt my chances of being accepted by society if I showed them too soon. It makes me a little sad because I do want to feel sexy sometimes. Or say "fuck" in a video.

"Hello?" Isadora answers the phone. "You know the rate for VIP, and it'll be more for everything. See you in an hour." She nonchalantly hangs up. "Dyl, come get ready with me, I need to put on some makeup. And I have a gift for you."

Tracey left to hit the bars and I went upstairs with Isadora to her hotel room. When I walked in, I nearly stepped on her teacup Pomeranian, who was the size of a grape. "You need to let me do your makeup one day. I'm amazing. We can make a video," Isadora proudly said as she sat down at the desk covered with every cosmetic

brand you could think of. I watched her contour, add
lashes, glitter, clipping in long blonde hair extensions;
she was pulling out all the stops. "Have you had
any celebrity men in your DMs yet?" she asked.

"No, just celebrity women looking for a friend."

"Huh . . . That's crazy. I can't keep up with them all in
my DMs."

"Wait, really?!" I was thrilled by this news. Oh my god,
does this mean I have a shot at kissing Timothée
Chalamet?

"Celebs love the dolls because they can have whatever
they want, so they get bored and then discover us.
Plus, we're discreet." She told me of two mega rappers
and an A-list actor who were recent clients. (So maybe
not the most discreet, but it's just us girls, right?)

"Just wait till you get your FFS, they'll be sliding in,"
she assured me. I had a hard time believing that these
men who were looking for discretion would message, let
alone sleep with, a trans TikToker who has a tendency
to tell the world everything. It did give me hope,
though, because maybe one of them will be confident
enough to publicly date someone like me one day.

"I almost forgot!" Isadora popped up from the
desk and ran over to her suitcase. "They're brand
new, don't worry." She flung a bag containing a
pink satin thong at me. "These are from my best
friend's company. They're the best for tucking."

They looked like a classic women's panty, but much sturdier. "Thank you! I've been wearing men's Calvin Klein briefs, so this is a definite step-up."

"Shut the fuck up. You're joking. Show me!" I hesitantly pulled my tights down to reveal my gray briefs. "Oh my god. Change those now." I went into the bathroom and put on the silk thong like any other undies. They were cute and comfy, but the bulge was still obvious. "Let's see 'em," coaxed Isadora from the other room.

I walked out and she jumped back up from the desk. "No, no, no, not like that." She pulled down her workout shorts and revealed a matching pair. "Like THIS!" And just like that . . . her undies were around her ankles and I was watching her pull her bits all the way between her legs. My Fairy Tuck Mother. "And make sure you pop up your balls way up inside toward your belly button. Your turn."

I started to walk toward the bathroom and got an "Oh come on. Show me!" I hadn't been naked in front of someone else for three and a half years other than bath times with Lily, and I didn't think the streak would be broken in a hotel room with my new trans friend, but one thing I am NOT is a prude. I did wish I had had a little warning so I could've shaved my pubes, but alas. I panty dropped in front of Isadora, and she coached me through. Once they were back on, my snatch was snatched! It was an extremely euphoric feeling. And like a bat out of hell, the hotel door burst open, and not with a gentleman caller. A blonde middle-aged trans woman rolled in her suitcase and collapsed on the couch.

"Oh my god, insane timing!" Isadora squealed and hugged the gal.

"Hey girl, oh god it's been a day," the woman said to me like we'd been friends for years.

"I'm Lina. What's your name?"

"I'm Dylan."

"Wait, you don't know who Dylan is?" said Isadora.

"Should I?" Lina looked at me with alarm.

"She's like . . . the TikTok girl."

"Oh! Well, I don't do any of that. I'm too busy running my own business."

"Lina makes the panties!" said Isadora, floating back to put makeup on.

"I don't make them, the factory does. I'm the CEO, bitch!" Lina exclaimed.

"I just hooked Dylan up with a pair. Dylan, show Lina the underwear you came in. Lina, you're gonna die."

I went to the bathroom and grabbed the Calvins off the floor, and meekly held them up like a painting that won last place in an art show.

"OH GIRL! BURN THOSE!" Lina exclaimed. "Did you not have any tucking panties before?"

"No, only these briefs," I said.

"You're in luck. I brought stock for Isadora and have a shit ton with me. I'll hook you up. And don't worry, you don't have to post about me or anything."

Lina opens her luggage to various colors and sizes. "What size are you wearing?" Lina asked me.

"I'm not sure," I replied. I discreetly pulled down my tights again to check the label.

Lina caught a glimpse of my tuck and said, "Oh for Christ's sake, you did it wrong."

She lifted up her dress and her panties dropped to the hotel room floor. Once again, I'm looking at yet another trans woman's bits.

"You need to pop the balls up before you tug, and make sure it's as far back as you can go," she directed as she demonstrated on herself. I adjusted mine simultaneously.

"See?! Much better. You're definitely an XS." I looked down and saw little to no difference in my tuck

than when Isadora coached me. Oh well, I suppose
a second Fairy Tuck Mother doesn't hurt.

"Here's seven pairs." She handed over a stack of
her inventory.

"That's way too generous! Let me pay you!"

"No, no. This is how I like to give back to our community,"
Lina said.

"Well then, why don't I just take two or three." I tried to
hand some back.

"But how are you going to get through a whole week?! I
am NOT letting you wear those god-awful briefs anymore.
Plus, mine work as bikini bottoms too. Just take them."

"Okay! Thank you times a million." I hugged her and felt
a deep sense of gratitude. Even if it was a peculiar
situation, it was very sweet.

"Ladies, he's almost here. Either stay and join or get
out." Isadora stood, now in lingerie and full beat. She
was beautiful, with curves in all the right places, long
hair, big lips, double D boobies. I quickly scanned her
body, wondering what parts of her I would want for
myself, and then remembered the paying customer about
to walk through the door.

"I'm gonna head out, but I had a really amazing time!"
I said as I gathered my new underwear and stuffed my
Calvins into my purse.

I walked out the door and headed to the elevator. I felt like I had just left a movie set. In the lobby, as I exited the elevator, a man was getting on. He was probably forty and decent looking. He didn't look my way, as he seemed to have somewhere to be. I wondered if that was the gentleman caller, and if it was, he was kind of my type. It was fun to think he might want to see me naked. Spending time with Isadora had renewed my sense of desirability.

Back at home I threw my new undies in the laundry hamper and went to clear out some of the briefs that I was told to burn. I had like thirty pairs, some dating back to high school. I plucked out most but kept the few that reminded me of specific hookups I had pre-transition. I realized I traded in my sexuality for self-proclaimed celibacy when I came out as trans. Tonight proved to me that I didn't have to. I have hope. Spending time with these dolls showed me just how valuable and necessary having trans women in my life is. As much as I've learned from cis women, the relationships and insights I can learn from other dolls will only help me grow in my version of womanhood.

I tossed the undies in the trash but kept four pairs of Calvin Klein underwear. Might be nice for a cozy, rainy day.

LOVE YA,

Dylan

Chapter 3

DYLAN! DOES! DISSOCIATION!

"Yep. Your cheek implant is infected. We're going to have to operate," says Dr. Lee in his Beverly Hills office. "Are you sure? I have some big events coming up that I can't miss." I attempt one last plea. "We can hold off for a little longer, but it's only going to get worse."

Fuck. My. Drag.

Since Beergate, it's been a pretty steady stream of shitstorms. What was once waking up to fairy-tale emails and invites to social engagements was now mornings filled with dread and more bad news. Today's drama: my infected cheek.

I had surgery six months ago, and the swelling from one of my cheek implants never went down. One side of my face was visibly puffier than the other, but nothing a little contour can't solve! It had gotten worse and worse leading up to Day 365, but the show took priority over my health. We spent weeks trying less aggressive ways to heal the infection, but now surgery was the only option. How was I supposed to schedule surgery and recover when I have paparazzi outside my door?! Oh Christ, the religious bigots are going to have a field day with this one. "Trans woman gets infection from botched plastic surgery, further proof that God hates her and Satan lives in her cheek."

Finding any ounce of joy after Beergate has been, well, a struggle. My other emotions were getting plenty of exercise: at the forefront was my anger toward conservative media and capitalism, followed by the fear of losing my career, and grief for the privacy I once had.

And of course there's my guilt over any potential setbacks to the trans community or god forbid violence, and, most strikingly, my sadness over the state of the world. My life coach, Mory, was working overtime, as I'd call her to extinguish daily fires I needed to put out. Lily was still around but had a husband at home and work to attend to, so she could only babysit me on occasion. A new confidant and friend emerged, Alok Vaid-Menon, who I looked up to immensely, and who would rationally teach me to navigate right-wing conservatives. But the one thing I wasn't sharing with any of them was my desire to no longer exist. To fade into nothingness. I've always hated asking for help, and even with my close loved ones I pride myself on being a light they can come to for entertainment or counsel. I did not want to burden them with my mental health mess. Which leads us to our next segment: DYLAN! DOES! DISSOCIATION!

* * * * *

Looking back on the aftermath of Beergate, I definitely should have gone away somewhere to get proper mental health treatment. I was so scared that news outlets would take my admission into a mental health facility as a way to paint me and all trans people as "psychos" who belong in the loony bin. How sad is it that we live in a time when seeking mental health resources is still so polarizing and shameful?! I assumed going away would be the nail in the coffin. I hadn't gotten a single brand deal since Beergate, and my existing deals were being put on hold or terminated. During that time, I had a few companies say, "You know what? No need to make content for us girlfriend, we'll just pay you out and call it a day." The IT Girl syndrome in me was still obsessed with trying to win back brand attention and find a place on the wheel of capitalism, but even more was my fear that I was no longer hirable for acting gigs, or even the longest love of my life,

Broadway. I feared that all the good progress I made in normalizing trans people in the media was taking a very ugly turn.

I had one brand deal that was still standing behind me proudly, a video with Lionsgate to interview beloved author Judy Blume for the new movie *Are You There God? It's Me, Margaret.* I convinced Dr. Lee to push out the cheek surgery in order to attend. I hadn't been out of the house in weeks, and I was so looking forward to meeting Judy. When I arrived early in the lobby of the Four Seasons where the press junket was taking place, I decided to freshen up in the women's restroom. What I was greeted with when I exited, or rather whom, took me by complete and utter shock.

"Dylan, what do you say to the women who are being raped by your kind in prison?!" A middle-aged man followed by his camera crew stuck a mic in my face. I didn't have any of my team members with me, and I ran straight to the front desk, where a young male worker was equally flustered. The journalist, if you could even call him that, continued to berate me with sickening questions, and he had zero shame. The only thing I could muster up to the Four Seasons worker was, "Please help me get to the movie press junket. Please."

In a daze, he escorted me to the elevator, where the journalist tried to get in with me, but the employee blocked him. The "journalist" yelled one last sick question before the door shut. I was pissed. "How did he even get in here?!" I ask the worker, who replied, "I have no idea how they got past security, it's trespassing for sure."

This confirmed to me that (a) these people were still on a Dylan witch hunt, and (b) they would do just about anything to get their content. Recently, I begrudgingly rewatched that video, because I wanted to be accurate for this essay, and I started crying because I can see the moment so clearly when I left my body and became a shell of myself. The "Dylan's not home right now" look behind my eyes simultaneously broke my heart and made me fume. And my infected cheek was quite obvious.

Disassociation to me feels like seeing Dylan Mulvaney as a character. Like a Sim. Instead of responding to a question, I'd think, *What would Dylan Mulvaney say to this?* It's looking in the mirror and your brain can't connect with what once was so clear.

I made it through the Judy Blume interview despite the frenzy just moments before. Judy Blume told me she was proud of me and that I had to keep going. It felt like such a stark representation of good and evil under the same roof. But to be honest, I wasn't really there.

* * * * *

The next night, I was hired to host the red carpet of the film. This was a huge career goal of mine, where I could show off my hosting skills alongside major stars with witty banter. I brought Lily as my date, along with two bodyguards (one got added due to the night before's antics). I thought everyone was being a little on edge, and I wanted a sense of normalcy. Though my team made it clear I didn't need to stay to watch the film, I was out on the town and ready to make a night of it. *Are You There God? It's Me, Margaret* is about a girl who is struggling to connect with a higher spiritual being, looking for answers to her problems and roadblocks in puberty. This hit me hard, because I too was looking up at the sky and wondering if there was anyone up there to help guide me through this mess. I feel close to God when the blessings rain down, but when the going gets tough, crickets. Why would God have let me take that beer contract if it was going to ruin me?

On the car ride home, Lily was being awkward and suspicious, which I had never felt from her in the sixteen years of our friendship. "What's going on?" I asked, as she was reading her texts. "Nothing," she responded. She was a terrible liar, so I did something I vowed I wouldn't do: I googled myself. I had made it a few weeks without looking up my name in an effort to cope with my depression, and her weirdness seemed like a good enough reason to break my streak.

"Beer factory faces bomb threats over Dylan Mulvaney advertisement, employees evacuated while SWAT team investigates."

My heart dropped. "Bomb threats?!" I yelled out. Lily, now trying to read my emotional state, said, "We didn't want to worry you while you were hosting the red carpet." I could tell she was genuinely scared and only wanted to protect me, but I also think I deserve to know when something this major happens. Why would someone blow up a beer factory for hiring a trans girl to do an Instagram video? Why wouldn't they just kill said trans girl instead and call it a day?

The car service and bodyguards dropped us off at my house, and I no longer had security with me overnight. Lily and I were left to our own devices: a kitchen knife and locks on the doors. We took one last best friend bath in my tub, as Lily was moving to London the next week with her British hubby. "Are you *sure* you're gonna be okay?" she called out behind a sea of Lush bubbles. "Yeah, I'll be fine. Just FaceTime me sometimes," I responded. We started a whirlpool, spinning our bodies around the jacuzzi tub like slick otters, naked but in the least sexual way possible. The edge of the tub caught my back and I pulled a muscle, so we topped the bath off with more hot water and relaxed. It felt safer in the bath for some reason, like if the murderers tried to get us our wet bodies would slip out of their grip.

Once Lily left, it was just me. My house that once felt like a Miss Honey cottage now felt more like a bunker. I really didn't want to move, but lack of privacy and the steepish rent made me question it. The last interior design touch that my decorator made was my wall of women in my bedroom. I chose twelve portraits of inspiring women I love with my whole heart: Frida Kahlo, Oprah, Miss Piggy, Marilyn Monroe, Marsha P. Johnson, Dolly Parton, Princess Diana, Michelle Obama, the casts of *The Golden Girls* and *Sex and the City*, Joni Mitchell, and, of course, Audrey Hepburn. Lying in my bed, I stare at these women, wondering what they would do if they caused a beer company to face bomb threats. I suspect Audrey Hepburn wouldn't have taken the offer in the first place but wouldn't judge me one bit.

* * * * *

The days turned to weeks and the weeks turned to months. This whole situation started to feel more and more like a video game that I was losing. Oh shit, I just lost the game. Do you remember the game? The only rule of the game was to not think about the game, and if you did think about it, you'd announce out loud, "I lost the game!" and everyone near you would also lose and start all over again. I started playing the game against my free will at age eleven backstage during the musical *You're a Good Man, Charlie Brown*. Sometimes years would go by when I didn't think about the game, just to lose randomly when I remembered it existed. My suicidal thoughts are kind of like my new game: How long can I go without wanting to die?

My desire to vanish into thin air was occurring multiple times a day. I would fall asleep thinking about not waking up, and how peaceful that sounded to me. I never had any intentions to act on these thoughts, but the peace and comfort I felt from them were deeply problematic. Death has never frightened me, because I've always been sure that I'll get to go home or feel cozy or heaven is a sea of opossums that I can pet whenever I want. As sad as some people would be to see me go, I also knew that it would bring joy to others. I was mostly attracted to the idea that I no longer would feel the weight of the world or the future of transness on my shoulders.

My mom came to stay with me for a few nights during this time, and she would crawl under the windows with the goal of not being seen by the paparazzi. An article titled "Who Are Dylan Mulvaney's Parents?" was released and they had gotten her confused with another Dana Mulvaney, so they reported that she was dead. This mistake thrilled my mom because that meant people wouldn't be hounding her the same way my dad was getting calls from strangers threatening him. Watching my mom crawl on the floor hiding from paparazzi is the last thing I would've ever expected out of life. It was so ridiculous that it almost couldn't be real. So, it wasn't. I decided that this was all some nightmare that I would wake up from and eventually I'd unpack life's lessons in the afterlife.

The scariest thing to happen during this chapter of my life was not death threats, or bomb squads, or canceled brand deals; the scariest thing was the numbness that took over my whole being. The emotions that once were so alive, although not positive but still present, eventually went silent. I was tired of fighting. I was majorly losing the game. I couldn't help but wonder if this would be easier for all involved if I just faded into nothingness. In moments of numbness, especially when lying motionless in bed on a difficult night, the small shred of fight left in me showed me there's love. I think about the trans kids in my DMs who came out to their parents because of me. I think of the Midwest moms in my comments section hyping me up like their own daughter. I think about Lily and our pledge to grow old together. These positive figures assemble an army against my Dark Thoughts.

While I was grateful for these saviors, I also wondered what they would think if they found out their favorite trans TikToker wasn't as happy as she appeared. That her heart was breaking and there were times that life felt so heavy that she wanted out of it. I look up at the women on my wall and know that if they felt that way, I would love them no less but would want them to stay to fight. So, I guess I should too.

DAY 90 of being a girl . . .

. . . And my mom came to visit. Dana lives just a few hours south of me in San Diego, but we don't see each other much based on a few factors.

When my parents divorced when I was nine, I emotionally sided with Dana. I saw Mom as the gatekeeper, and my dad as the one I asked for permission from only when Mom said "no" first. His response usually was "Ask your mother." My mom quickly married a cowboy named Larry—we moved in with Larry to his ranch house with dead animals on the wall. My relationship with Dana was sweet and codependent until my puberty set in. If I had guessed which parent would've had the more difficult time accepting me, on paper I would have chosen my dad. He's straight as can be and lacks emotional depth in the way straight dads sometimes do. What I didn't realize was that lack of emotional depth was actually working in my favor—unlike my mom, who could talk about feelings for hours accompanied by plenty of tears.

We had our tiffs through my early teens, usually surrounding my appearance. When I bleached my hair, she made me dye it back the next day. (God, people really wanted to keep me from accessing the power of blonde.) When I had clear nail polish on, emphasis on CLEAR, she pulled out the acetone. When she found out I was attending the Pride parade as a fourteen-year-old, she drove around until she found me on the street in my tiny short-shorts and nearly dragged me out by the ear.

Our biggest blowout happened my freshman year of high school, when she read through my texts while I was in the shower. Remember Boy Scout Billy? Yeahhhh. I opened the bathroom door to her raccoon eyes wet with tears. She shook the phone in my face. "YOU'RE IN A

SEXUAL RELATIONSHIP WITH AN ADULT MAN?!" She
shook the cellphone so hard that a boob fell out of
her robe.

"Okay lady, calm down—he's eighteen not fifty, his name
is Billy, we've only kissed, and he's an Eagle Scout for
Christ's sake! Now put that tit away!" . . . is what I
should have said at that moment, but instead I ran
away to my dad's.

I didn't speak to my mom for weeks—the only time we'd
see each other was in a therapy session. As a child, I was
always vocal when I felt like I needed mental support,
and my parents always addressed my needs. I had been
seeing a psychiatrist for depression for a few months
leading up to this. When I went silent with my mom, she
joined me for a few sessions with my psychiatrist, who
played mediator. Dana spent most of our sessions sobbing
about how scared she was for the hardships I would have
to endure as a gay man, and how she was nervous about
what her friends and family would think about us, both
her and me. I was so fed up with this, to the point
where one day I stopped her and said, "If you can't
accept me at this moment, all of me, you are not my
mother anymore."

I felt like such a bad bitch, 'cause I meant it, but also
really guilty for the harshness. She stopped crying.
It was almost as if she got spiritually slapped in
the face. "Okay, okay. Fine," is all she said. Dana
knew I meant it too.

My Mother's Ideal Version of a Gay Son

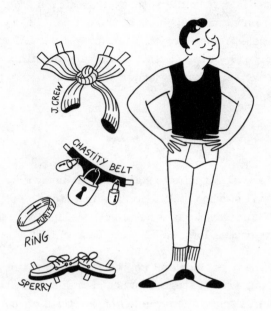

From then on, I was "allowed" to be gay as long as I lived up to her version of idyllic faggotry.

After marrying Larry the cowboy, my mom joined one of those rock band-type modern churches and would drag me with her. Picture "Our God Is an Awesome God" followed by a pastor in cowboy boots whispering sweet nothings, building up to a full Broadway belt of multilevel marketing energy. I will never forget the service when off-brand Joel Osteen told everyone the story of a baker turning down a gay couple's cake and the baker getting villainized by the media. "We must protect our families from this war on marriage," he told the church. So, my mom took home a "Yes on Prop 8" sign for our yard. I will never forget looking at that sign every morning. It made me feel like my mother's love, and God's, was conditional.

* * * * *

I do not say all of this to make you think my mom was an evil swamp witch. I don't want today to be Shit on Dana Day. I say it because I really love her, and we've come a long way. It gets better! Ish!

Once I went to college and we had some separation, we entered our friend stage. The best part of this stage was when I turned twenty-one and we could have a drink together. She would visit me at college in Cincinnati and we bar crawled and hit the casino. Dana started leaning in to cool mom energy, but every now and then would still revert back to judgmental mom energy. I remember one night lying in my college bedroom together, and she asked, "Have you ever smoked pot?"

"Yeah, I have," I said calmly, my guard down since she felt like a BFF.

"WELL, THAT'S HORRIBLE! Dylan . . . it's horrible for you." She totally sobered me up.

She quickly reminded me she was my mother and not my
best friend, even though the roles sometimes weren't
clear. It was always a balancing act with her;
how much I could share without saying too much.
We were growing, but there were still pains.

When I came out as nonbinary two years ago, she
didn't attempt to use my pronouns. At a small family
get-together, I constantly was misgendered, which
felt like little BB gun pellets hitting my gut. I struggled with the guilt of forcing this on them, coupled
with the pain of knowing they didn't see me the way
I wanted.

And ninety days into my Girlhood series, my mom and
I hadn't seen each other in person yet. The thought
of sharing my womanhood with the woman who
birthed me was the most intimidating of them all.
Would my womanhood be a slap in the face to hers?

Anytime an exciting opportunity came around these
last couple of months, I would call my mom first. I
was constantly seeking her validation. The millions
of followers didn't hold a candle to the desperation
I felt for my mother's unconditional love.

TikTok named me a "Trailblazer" for the month of June.
As soon as I found out, I called my mom to tell her the
news. On top of that title, TikTok also put me up on a
billboard on Sunset Boulevard. I live just a five-minute
walk away, so in moments of sadness, it was a quick

pick-me-up to walk by and feel special. It's one of those digital screens, so it rotates every few seconds, but if you catch it at the right moment, there's my trans mug smiling! My mom was very impressed by the billboard, enough for her to schedule a trip up to come see the billboard and me in person. I was giddy and scared.

Some days I have been grasping at straws to make a daily video. So, I thought a video with my mom, if she was willing, would be PERFECT. We could talk about femininity, motherhood, my early years, the options are endless. I called Dana last night to run this by her, and she said, "I . . . just don't know. Let me sleep on it." I took that as a hard yes. I'm pretty convincing, so I assumed I could warm her up when she arrived.

Today I put on the pinkest Y2K outfit I own, thinking that the more feminine I appeared, the less likely she'd misgender me. Dana arrived at my little studio apartment, and I immediately started pitching content ideas.

A Conversation with My Mom

Me: Okay, so, I've been thinking about our video, and I think we can make it short and sweet.

My mom hesitated.

Mom: I called my therapist on the drive up here, and he thinks you might be pushing me to do this too fast.

Me: Mom, people keep asking me about my family, and I want to make you look good. Wouldn't you rather we control the narrative instead of the media? We can show my followers that you are supportive and on the right side of things.

I reasoned, a little desperately.

Mom: But what if I don't support everything you're doing? What if I don't agree with it all?

Another BB bullet to the gut. I hadn't considered that she maybe doesn't want to be associated with my very public life. The only reason I still have Facebook is to check if my mom has shared anything of mine or the press I've gotten. When I visit her profile, I'm greeted with photos of my half-siblings and her grandkids, but I'm nowhere in sight. What would be enough to be featured in her life?

"Well, let's walk to the billboard, I guess. And maybe we can do a video there if you feel up for it. No pressure, though," I told her. I hadn't made a backup plan for today's video. My delusional self hadn't even considered that she wouldn't appear.

We walked along Sunset Boulevard in silence, so much unsaid, but neither of us wanted to ruin the moment. My mom was planning on staying over, so I was prepping for a long, possibly awkward day. As we neared the billboard, I asked, "How about just a little cameo and I'll make the video about the billboard and not you?"

"Okay," she responded.

I started filming and felt a trickle of shame pouring over me, feeling my mom's eyes on my back while I imagined her judgments. When I flipped the camera to her, I asked, "What's your favorite part of girlhood?"

"Spa days," she quietly let out.

Same, girl . . . Same. I can understand the safety in coasting on an answer that feels surface or materialistic. Much easier than unpacking femininity on camera with your twenty-six-year-old newly trans daughter. I was thrilled that she even made the attempt.

We got to the billboard right as my face projected for a few seconds. Then a car ad.

"Was that it?"

"Yeah. It'll come back in a minute or two."

We made small talk through two or three more rounds and then called it.

"Pretty cool!" she said, with an awkward undertone.

Maybe the billboard I actually craved was a simple photo on her Facebook page, not a giant sign over Sunset Boulevard. I edited the video while we walked home, and she stopped to watch it.

"God, I look heavy," she said.

"No, you look amazing! This is gonna make my followers love you. And you don't have to make another appearance."

"Okay, fine."

I hit post. And I was right. The positive comments immediately began to flood in.

The validation from the commenters, even referring to my and my mom's fifteen seconds of interaction, felt weirdly good. Maybe if my followers believed I had a wildly supportive family, it would be true.

we STAN Dana

Need more mom content

So glad you have a safe support system!

When we got back to my apartment, I realized I had Zoom therapy, which I could take in the car, unless . . . "Are open to joining?" I asked my mom.

"I don't know."

"You could just, say, introduce yourself for a second?"

"Alright."

It really may sound like I'm inappropriately pushing, but I know that my mom won't seek out resources if I don't pressure her into a little progress. The more she has to acknowledge me as a trans person, whether that's online or in private, the more real it becomes. Seeing her so sparingly, I knew today was a rare opportunity for growth. So, I tried to fit years of resources and healing into this one day.

We popped onto Zoom, where my therapist, Andrew, was surprised to see two people. He'd always been excited about the idea of a group session with my family, but I hadn't prepped him. Oops.

A Conversation Surprising My Therapist

Me: So sorry to spring this on you, here's my mom!

Andrew: No worries at all, nice to meet you!

Mom: I'm only staying for a second.

That second turned into an hour, just like I knew it would. We talked about our relationship over the years and how it's evolved, and what codependent habits we still have left over. When we took a dive back into my childhood, she began sharing anecdotes about me growing up that I had never even heard. Stories about me talking about my gender, or using the wrong bathroom in kindergarten, and my obsession with Barbies. I could tell she was allowing herself to start connecting the dots. The information was invaluable to me as well, because there were things coming up that predated my own memory. These stories were the greatest gift she could've ever given me.

Of course, the tears came, especially at the end of our session, when she said, "I feel like I'm grieving my son." This made my heart break, because I realized I wasn't allowing her the time she needed to adjust. It would have been epic to have a mom who understood my transness immediately and had Pride flags up on her porch, but I don't. I also don't have a mom who kicked me out for my queerness, which is a win in my book. I don't want to settle for less than I deserve, but maybe my worth can be met with time and care.

"That's unfortunately all the time we have," Andrew told us. My mom and I both had tears rolling down our cheeks. We had only just skimmed the surface of our relationship.

"No worries. I'll see you next week. Bye!" And with that, I ended the Zoom with a man I've never met in person but has so so so much good tea on me.

"I think we deserve a glass of wine!" my mom joked.

"I think so too!" I agreed.

✳ ✳ ✳ ✳ ✳

Back to our lighthearted banter, the awkwardness is gone. After a glass of wine and my mom complaining about the dirt on my baseboards for the eighth time, we walked to a sports bar on Sunset for dinner. She ordered ribs and more wine, and I ordered the mac and cheese.

The server stopped writing in her pad. "Oh my god, are you the girl from TikTok?" she asked me.

"Yes, I am."

"Hold on . . ."

My mom's brows raised. Moments later the server returned with two shots, both lit on fire.

"I love your videos so much. Hope you like tequila!" she exclaimed.

"I do!" I smiled. I don't actually, I'm allergic, remember? But it's the thought that counts. And, besides, my mom loves tequila.

"Wow, does that happen a lot?" my mom asked.

"Sometimes. Especially if I'm somewhere gay or with lots of women."

"I think I like the perks! I gotta call your aunt Peggy and tell her what happened, she'll die," my mom said as she began sipping her shot. I poured mine into my water glass so I didn't appear rude. Thank you to that waitress, wherever you are, you were integral in getting me a little bit closer to Dana's approval.

My mom left the next day, and although we weren't magically healed by a billboard with my face on it, or a TikTok that did well, or an amazing therapy session . . . our relationship changed. For the better. A little bit. And that little bit was enough for me to keep calling her with the good news.

LOVE YA,

Dylan

DAY 98 of being a girl . . .

. . . And I'm headed on a family vacation. It's my mom's birthday weekend, and her big wish was to have all her kids together, so I put my nerves aside to indulge her. Only my mom's side is coming, since obvi my dad's not tagging along—he's had two wives since Dana. I'm driving to Palm Springs, California, to meet up with my mom, her husband, Larry, my older half-siblings, Stacey and Brett, and Brett's wife, Lulu, and their three kids. This will be the first time the family would see me in my true identity in person. I probably should've eased in with a casual meal, but I'm looking at an entire weekend full of either (a) awkwardness or (b) TRANS 101.

Whenever someone starts asking me questions about my transition, I think of myself as Professor Mulvaney and I'm teaching TRANS 101. When the questions become more complex or confrontational, I think of that as TRANS 201 and so on, which I don't feel equipped yet to handle.

- Are you changing your name?

- Are you still attracted to men?

- Will you get the surgery?

If you suspect your question for a trans person is inappropriate, it probably is. I am a pretty open book and tend to answer honestly if the person asking seems sincere and safe. I wasn't sure if my family was going to proceed business as usual, or if the TRANS 101 classroom would be in session.

When I arrived at the hotel, it was almost dark but still over 100 degrees outside. Palm Springs in the summer is no joke. I got a message from the rarely used family group chat telling me to come out to the pool.

My family + me in a women's swimsuit = jump scare. So,
I set my things in the hotel room I'm sharing with my
sister Stacey and walk outside in a dress so that it's
clear I wouldn't be swimming. I found everyone out by
the pool already lounging, Lulu was packing up the
kids' toys, and my mom jumped up. "OOOOH so good to see
you! I've got all my kids with me!" She looked genuinely
happy. I hugged everyone, except for Larry, who I gave
a friendly wave to. Larry would be the biggest anxiety
for me this weekend. It's not like Larry and I would
erupt in fighting words, since we hadn't done that since
I was twelve on a cruise to the Caribbean. (I wanted to
visit the late-night dessert bar and got cranky with
my mom when she wouldn't let me. Larry stepped in and
yelled at me about it. I cried. But it's not like I'm
holding on to that or anything . . .) I mostly wondered
what he was going to be thinking on the inside.

I figured I was safe with the rest of my family. Stacey,
thirty-nine, is super sweet and has always been
supportive of me, but sometimes my mom tries to rope
her in on judgments of me with a classic "Well, Stacey
thinks so too," when she needs the backup. Brett,
thirty-six, is bro-ish on the outside, goofy on the
inside, and I think will be okay with me too. I recently
found out he officiated a lesbian wedding, which is
giving ally. He and my mom were distant with each
other when he was in his late teens and I was little,
so we didn't bond much as kids, but we've had our
share of fun since I turned twenty-one. Brett loves
to crack jokes, so we connect over comedy. Lulu, his

wife, is sweet and I assume will be intrigued about the reality TV stars I've met. Then there are Brett and Lulu's kids, three, one, and one, who are probably too young to even know that I was a boy in the first place. Kinda cool that they'll only know girl Dylan.

After our pool hang, we all met up for dinner in the hotel dining room. The drinks were flowing but the conversation stayed surface. After we covered the usual topics of weather, jobs, and kids, Lulu threw me a bone. "So, tell us what Kathy Hilton is like!" she exclaimed halfway through entrees. Telling my family about the industry was fun, because it felt like currency with them. Like I earn a seat at the table if my stories have entertainment value. I told them about getting my hair done by JVN last week and signing with a big talent agency yesterday. Everyone asked questions except Larry.

After dinner, the girls (including me, eeee!) went back to mine and Stacey's for champagne and chatting. As we popped the cork, I pulled out the immunity idol *For the* I brought with me: free PR swag bags for all three *Survivor girlies* of the gals. My mom, Stacey, and Lulu all went around pulling out one item at a time—unused MAC lipsticks I got to keep from our collab, entire skin-care lines that I was too afraid of trying on my sensitive skin, and I even threw in a few tampons. The ladies traded products with each other like kids bartering Halloween candy. It was so fun to watch. I felt like I added value in this family, as shallow as that value might be.

A Conversation with Lulu

Me: This contour palette works great. It's super feminizing and helpful until I get FFS.

Lulu: What's FFS?

Class is in session.

Me: Facial feminization surgery. It's going to soften all my features. I think it makes sense to start with this one since I'm so public-facing, then maybe my boobs next year . . . and besides, I can't consider bottom surgery yet anyways. I haven't been on hormones long enough.

Lulu: Oh wow! How does that surgery work?

I spent the next ten minutes explaining the different bottom surgery techniques and who the best doctors were according to the internet.

"And I should still be able to orgasm. I've heard it's amazing," I added for dramatic flair.

My mom was clearly uncomfortable, and this started well before the orgasm comment. Hearing her child talk about shifting around their looks and genitalia wasn't the easiest thing. Half of me felt bad for her, and the other half felt satisfied because I was an adult and she couldn't stop me from doing what I knew was right for me. I laid off the TRANS 101 after that last answer because it was my mom's birthday after all. We all scattered off to bed.

"See you at the pool bright and early!" my mom said as she left the room.

Oh god.

Pool.

* * * * *

The next morning, I woke up hungover and dreading the idea of myself in a bikini next to my fam. Millions of people had seen me in a bathing suit over the last few months on TikTok, but funny how this feels more intimidating than that. I debated which swimsuit to wear, weighing the pros and cons of each.

Dylan's Bathing Suit Pros/Cons

- My Burberry is a one-piece, which feels safe and nonthreatening, but my boobs look completely flat and the tuck isn't super easy.

- The H&M bikini was pretty skimpy but looked good with my skin tone and didn't show my butt.

- The swim trunks from pre-transition and a workout bra were the safest option but felt like a death to my whole brand.

I went with the H&M bikini. Lucky that Lina had gifted me those tucking panties—they fit perfectly under the lavender bottoms and my crotch looked decently flat. To the pool I go.

It was 102 degrees when I walked up to greet the group, and I was the last to arrive yet again.

The air was so dry and hot that getting in the pool was the only ticket to relief. I also realized that if my crotch was underwater people would have a harder time clocking it. I made sure to never submerge my face or neck, in fear that my makeup would run off, revealing my beard shadow. Oh, the mental gymnastics of a trans girl! Larry sat on his chair with a beer, and I briefly made eye contact with him. I couldn't think of a world where this wasn't absolutely wild for him to see. A hunting, fishing electrician and a lavender bikini-wearing trans girl hanging by the pool. Sounds like a fun Hallmark movie. I found my brother and his kids in the children's pool and spent the afternoon hanging with him, watching my nephew go down the tiny slide over and over again.

There was one big waterslide, and waterslides happen to be one of my top favorite things, just behind Jacuzzis and just in front of sour candy.

Dylan's Favorite Things Pyramid

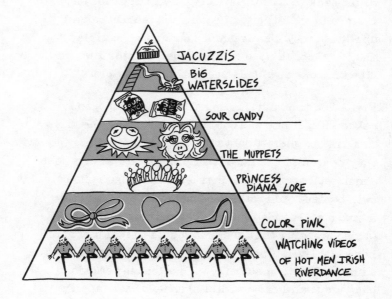

I went back and forth deciding if I should risk wet hair to live out my slide fantasy. *Fuck it.* I climbed the steps and waited in line with the people ahead of me. My dream is to one day become the eighty-year-old grandma waiting in the waterslide line. I got to the front, lay down like a mummy, and did one last look at my bikini bottoms to make sure I was still situated correctly. I closed my eyes and twisted down. The slide itself ended up being kind of a dud, but my tucking panties were still in place. SUCCESS!

Back in our room, Lulu brought the kids to come say goodbye, since I was going to be leaving early. (I had to get back to LA for Day 100.) Now in dry clothes, I hung out with the twin babies while Lulu caught up with Stacey. I sang Disney songs to the girls, and they looked up at me in wonder. I think I would like kids one day. We'll see if that's possible.

I realized that I still needed a day 99 video, so I asked Lulu if she was cool with me putting the girls in a TikTok where I babysat them. "Totally! Oh my god they're going to be famous!" My mom and I always joke about getting them into commercials because identical twin babies could make good money in Hollywood. I filmed a silly video making babysitting jokes, and I was so grateful that she allowed me to feel a part of her kids' lives. I packed up my physical baggage and said goodbye to the family with a lot less emotional baggage than I came with. Maybe we *could* happily coexist. Maybe I could drive down to San Diego and

show face at family events more often. Maybe I'm not
the monster I assumed they saw me as. Maybe they
love me more unconditionally than I believed. I
deserved an In-N-Out milkshake after all this.

I grab a milkshake and get the hell out of that hot, hot
town. Back to LA for day 100!

LOVE YA,

Dylan

DAY 100 of being a girl . . .

. . . And I'm exhausted. I cannot believe I just made 100 videos in 100 days.

These past few months have felt like a fever dream that I keep expecting to wake up from, alone and drenched in sweat. I keep worrying that this will all be gone. But every morning, I am greeted by a few thousand more people saying hello, wishing me well on my transition, and anxiously awaiting the next *Days of Girlhood* video. The part of me that is most shocked by this 100-videos-in-100-days conquest is the ADHD-ridden version of myself who loves to lie in bed all day. I am proud that I wrestled with her until we could achieve our goal. But no time to get too comfy, we need today to be BIG.

I am supposed to meet with my therapist today, but I have to cancel yet again. I've tried to keep up with my therapy appointments with my queer therapist, Andrew, but I find myself canceling them for last-minute opportunities that I can't pass up. When I do make it to a session, I spill a mile a minute to Andrew, and he stares at me for twenty-five minutes until I finally stop talking. I try to fit all gender introspection into this one hour of the week. It's reminiscent of Sundays in church confession growing up. I find myself asking him for help outside of my identity, more specific to celebrity, and he tries his best to give me his take but shares that he doesn't have a lot of experience with this world. He also says he doesn't watch my content because it's a privacy violation, but I find that hard to believe. I've told him multiple times that it probably would help our sessions so I don't have to give him as much context, but he still resists. My desire to have him watch my videos is to further convince him that I'm happy. I want him to see me smiling on the screen, the same way my followers take me in, so that I don't have to explore the real vulnerability of therapy. Sorry for canceling today, Andrew!

In some ways, today is a celebration for my followers more than it is for me—I can enjoy later. My first video to post is a collection of videos sent in from my celeb pals and TikTok mutuals all ringing in Day 100. The second video was my merch shirts announcement, which made me feel a little used-car-salesman-ish, but the shirts turned out cute. For the third video I planned to meet a follower out in the wild.

One of the oddest parts of this whole chapter of my life has been the lack of connection to real humans. Sure, I see friends and mutuals at parties, but most of the time I'm alone in my room talking to people I've never met and possibly never will. I want to change that, at least a little for today, by finding some followers in the flesh. So, I went from my photoshoot to the place I knew would have ample gays and teen girls roaming: the Grove. I set up my tripod right outside Wetzel's Pretzels on a strip of grass and got a few puzzled looks. The Grove is a natural habitat for influencer content, but I still felt awk. Sure, I grew up performing on stages, but those audiences had chosen to be there. The mall pedestrians of the Grove did not buy a ticket to the Dylan Show, so I was fully aware of how cringe this could be. I powered through because I'm used to doing things that scare me.

I had free merch shirts and hundred-dollar bills to give to followers if they approached me. After a few minutes without anyone walking up, I started to have a panic-thought, *Maybe all the people in my phone weren't actual humans and I was the most delusional person on the planet?* Seconds later, the cutest sisters sheepishly approached me asking me if I was Dylan. I exclaimed YES and scooped them up in a group hug. I gave the sisters their prizes, and it felt serendipitous.

After greeting a few more new friends, I needed sustenance, so I hit up Wetzel's Pretzels. The gal working the register, Creeda, recognized me and said the pretzel was on her. The pretzel made me feel like I really made it. I hope the limelight always tastes this good. As I thanked her profusely, Creeda ran out of the kiosk and we took a photo together. Now when I go to make a video for millions of strangers, I'll at least know Creeda is watching.

On my way home from the Grove, I swung by my local Cold Stone and picked up a custom Birthday Cake Remix ice cream cake. Cold Stone cakes are a much rarer treat than a Domino's deep pan—I usually reserve them exclusively for my birthday. But today kind of felt like my birthday, so I'm making an exception. When I got home, I hopped into my canopy bed and took a fork straight into the cake for one last video. I filmed my bite, posted, and then sighed.

I scrolled through comments from my internet friends, smiling as I read. My dopamine was out of control, but it wasn't until I looked down at the melting cake that I realized there was no one there in real life to help me eat it.

I think most trans girls who are celebrating a transition milestone might have invited their loved ones or other doll friends over, and that thought makes me a little sad. I've been prioritizing the people on my screen more than the humans in my life, and if that doesn't change soon, it could lead to regret. This would've been helpful to unpack in my canceled therapy appointment. I put the cake in the freezer so that I could have it for breakfast tomorrow. I couldn't wait to sleep in and maybe skip making a video. You did it Dyl. Wooo.

LOVE YA,

Dylan

100 THINGS I'VE LEARNED IN 100 DAYS OF GIRLHOOD

1. One boob will grow faster than the other—
   we can only pray they'll even out.

2. You shouldn't straighten wet hair. *Tsssszzzsssssz*

3. Tampons come in multiple sizes.

4. Content creation is a FULL-time gig.

5. Filming yourself alone in public feels
   absolutely batshit, and I cringe every time.

6. Once you reach a certain level of success, people
   from your past will come out of the woodwork
   and into your orbit. Be careful who you let in.

7. Yellow and orange are not really my colors.

8. Pink and blue *are* my colors.

9. I might want to dye my hair blonde?

10. The higher up a piercing is on your
    ear, the longer it takes to heal.

11. Serving a new look every day is an
    impossibly high (and expensive) bar to set.

12. Acrylics will mess up your nails.
    Bad. But they just hit so good.

13. **Not everyone's willing to date a trans person.**

14. Calvin Klein briefs do not work
    as tucking panties.

15. **Powder your orange color corrector
    before applying concealer on top of it.**

16. Brand partnerships pay infinitely
    higher than Broadway contracts and
    require infinitely less work.

17. **Sleepovers are an excellent time to use
    your friends' phones to stalk exes.**

18. Going viral is great way to hear from your
    sixth-grade bullies.

19. **Driving alone with a stranger in an Uber can be
    extremely anxiety-inducing.**

20. Jumpsuits don't work for my torso.

21. **There is nothing healthy about
    making 100 videos in a row.**

22. There is nothing healthy about disclosing your
    most vulnerable moments on the internet.

23. **Laser hair removal will not
    work after one session.**

24. My singing voice has largely remained the same.
    A little drier, a little airier, but I've still got it.

25. **Auditioning for female characters has
    made me re-fall in love with acting.**

26. I still prefer men's razors over women's.

27. **Crying directly to camera on the internet feels cathartic at first and then absolutely embarrassing shortly after.**

28. A little bit of delusion goes a long way.

29. **When you unlock your proper gender identity, your horoscope hits that much harder.**

30. Women know exactly what to say to hit you where it hurts.

31. **It's deceivingly difficult to style hair.**

32. There's a fridge in Wisconsin with my sperm on ice.

33. **Allies are so afraid of offending trans people that they often won't offer constructive criticism.**

34. Chicken cutlet titties need to be replaced every three uses.

35. **Now that I'll be the bride, my family is supposed to pay for the wedding. (My dad said, "Love you but no.")**

36. Broadway doesn't know how to accommodate trans performers (yet).

37. **For us coarse-haired girlies, eyebrow threading should be scheduled every two and a half weeks unless you're going for the Eugene Levy look.**

38. Even when you don't feel like hot shit, know your worth, because one day you *will* be hot shit.

39. **Your dress size varies from store to store. Don't pay too much attention.**

40. A wedged heel will always be more comfortable than a stiletto.

41. Picking up the tab will always feel good unless the person at the other end of the table expects you to.

42. Chivalry is not dead, it's just on life support. (I gotta say, though, having the door opened for you does feel really nice.)

43. I never knew what I was missing until estrogen made my nipples sensitive, and now I'll never look back.

44. A man can switch from adoration to anger in a second if he's not getting what he wants.

45. No matter the tucking situation, waterslides will ALWAYS be worth it.

46. There's no better stand-up show in LA than in the backyard of a lesbian's house in Eagle Rock (where the cool kids live).

47. Twenty hours of screen time a day is too much.

48. Meeting your heroes is excellent . . . 90% of the time.

49. My moon is in Virgo and my ascendant is in Pisces.

50. Internal validation will always feel better than the external, but when the external gets loud, that tends to take the cake. Take the external with a grain of salt.

51. My happiest moments are when I have zero expectations and a thousand pleasant surprises.

52. My saddest moments are when I let people who don't know me dictate the way I think of myself.

53. Brussels sprouts aren't that bad if they're fried.

54. Waving on a Pride float *is* exactly as fun as you'd imagine.

55. A problematic brand will offer you an exorbitant amount of money to promote their product, and saying "no" will feel good. Feel empowered to say no.

56. Don't underestimate the intelligence of your audience.

57. I'm telling ya, one boob is going to grow faster than the other.

58. Maternal affection always reigns supreme.

59. There's a big difference between asking and telling. The older I get, the more telling I do, so when I do ask questions, they hold more weight.

60. Listening to music from a female perspective hits that much harder.

61. Cockroaches in West Hollywood are inevitable.

62. Bottle service is a real thing. I still don't understand who's paying for it, but I'm happy to indulge.

63. Opera gloves add a touch of class to any outfit, and you're less self-conscious about the size of your arms.

64. Heart-shaped sunglasses go with everything.

65. Apparently, there are whole weeks dedicated to fashion?

66. Candles are really expensive.

67. Invest in a steamer: The steam of an outfit before you walk out the door can take you from a seven to an eleven.

68. Don't mix silicone- and water-based makeup products.

69. Ease into flirting, don't interrogate a man who you just met at a bar.

70. Who needs a camera operator when you have a selfie stand and a purse-sized ring light.

71. Wear a button-down or robe while doing your makeup so you don't have to pull a T-shirt over your head and risk ruining everything.

72. The women's bathroom may not be as glam as anticipated, but it smells much better.

73. Keep your hormones on your bedside table so that when you come home from a long night and are too tired to take your makeup off you still pop your estrogen.

74. Despite trying a thousand new things, I'm still completely uninterested in trying healthier foods.

75. Moms are just grown-up daughters.

76. Dads can get it right eventually.

77. PR boxes make for great birthday gifts.

78. There aren't as many bad apples in Hollywood as you'd expect, but when you do come across one of those bad apples, they are blatantly rotten. Toxicity is hard to hide.

79. **I didn't realize how few women are in power until I found myself in rooms where I was the only woman present.**

80. My bladder has gotten leakier the longer I've been on estrogen.

81. **I get to look forward to prostate AND mammogram exams.**

82. The look that your best friend gives you waking up from a sleepover is exactly the same even after you change identities.

83. **Schedule at least an hour to attempt a red lip. Keyword: Attempt.**

84. A pinky nude lip is always the safest choice.

85. **The tabloids are even more toxic in the UK, and for some reason, they're interested in trans TikTokers in America.**

86. There is a Carole King song for every occasion.

87. **There is also a Joni Mitchell song for every occasion.**

88. Business class is addictive, so find someone else who can pick up the tab.

89. **I spend more time editing TikTok videos than I do sleeping.**

90. Flowers from Trader Joe's can really turn a day around.

91. **Not enough people celebrate canopy beds for adults.**

92. Doing the right thing isn't always easy.

93. **Lip filler migrates.**

94. A quarter-life crisis isn't always such a bad thing.

95. ***Golden Girls* and queso while stoned is the recipe for a perfect night in.**

96. Therapists aren't God.

97. **Everyone has a podcast.**

98. It's amazing how productive you can be when you're not stoned!

99. **Dirty Shirley Temples make for a wicked hangover.**

100. No but seriously: ONE BOOB *WILL* GROW FASTER.

Chapter 4

CONFESSIONS OF A
CATHOLIC SCHOOL GIRL

Months after Beergate, I'd fallen far from my IT Girl throne and lost control of my emotions. I was rarely getting out of bed, looking for ways to lash out, turning away from the world. The last time I felt this way was as a teenager.

Up until high school, despite being a grown woman in a little twink's body, my innocence was still intact. I would hang out with my mom or dad willingly and surf playbill.com instead of Pornhub, and finding a B on my report card was damn near impossible. I was a total teacher's pet. Catholic school added an extra opportunity to suck up: by reading the Bible out loud in front of my two thousand classmates at Cathedral Catholic High School masses. (Potentially the most uncool thing I could've done.) The guilt I felt surrounding my queerness made me put in extra effort so I could make it up to Jesus, or God, or whoever controlled the karma over my sins. One of the main spaces I could really repent was in confession, which is a sacrament where you tell your sins to a priest in a little room off the side of a church, he absolves you of said sins, and then you go and pray a couple of Hail Marys and you're g2g. Unless your sins are SO bad that he can't "absolve" them.

This particular day, fourteen-year-old me walked into the church with the song of Catholic guilt in my heart, which sounds exactly like the *Jaws* theme song. Slowly the devil had been taking me over to give in to my "shameful" desires. I knew something needed to be done after a group sleepover at Mary Grace's house when I rolled around making out with upperclassman hottie Ace (who I had been eyeing since August) while everyone was still sleeping. It didn't help that the next day when I texted him about our secret affair, he responded with "I don't know what you're talking about." Gay Catholic guilt, party of two. My queerness was weighing on me more than ever, and I thought maybe sharing my struggle with the priest would offer some comfort and guidance. I started with the easy stuff, running through my more trivial sins like cursing or disrespecting my parents, and then saved the big one for last:

"I have sinned, for I am gay, or at least, I am attracted to men, and I've felt this for a long, long time . . . I am sorry," I whispered through the mesh window next to me.

The priest paused for what felt like an eternity, and finally said, "I can absolve the rest, but the last, I cannot. I wish you well on your journey and take care of yourself."

Did the priest feel that I was such a lost cause that there was no point in even attempting to fix me?! I didn't even tell him about the tonsil hockey I played at that sleepover or the half hand job I gave over the summer! I walked out of the church that day with a new song in my heart: defiance. I knew of other friends whose sins were far worse than being gay and had been absolved. I did everything right, and this one Catholic caveat made me no good!?! For the rest of my time at Catholic school, I made it my mission to reject any and all signs of faith. Frequently being bullied or mocked by freshman boys made it clear that there was no God looking out for me. Fun fact: I did whip out my can of hairspray to spray in one of my bully's faces when he tried to rough me up in the locker room. He never picked on me ever again, and my hair was so stiff that a football couldn't have made a dent.

Slowly, I started finding comfort in femininity, like using makeup, which was strictly against the school's handbook for boys. When a librarian tried to confront me for the obvious cakey paint on my face, I replied, "Oh this? It's a tinted prescription medication for acne from my dermatologist. If you have a problem with it, I'd happily connect you with my doctor." Without missing a damn beat.

The last straw was . . . *dance team.* The only thing that could've brought me any semblance of joy at that school was the infamous dance team, which performed slightly sexy little numbers at every football and basketball halftime show. I practiced for that goddamn dance audition for WEEKS. When it finally came time, I sissy-ed my way across the floor, just to be rejected as a team member. NOT EVEN JUNIOR VARSITY?! This was the last straw in my Jesus milkshake, and the whole experience sent me into a fury. **Cue: "World Burn" from the musical *Mean Girls.***

* * * * *

Destination: Planet Bad Girl. First stop? Transfer to the weird, artsy public school. Time to burn my beige dockers and find the children of liberals.

Second Stop: Quit theater. No one would take my rebellion seriously if I was still Fosseing my way across a stage, so I made the conscious decision to stop auditioning. My new public school had a great theater program, but I knew that if I had continued performing, I would have been confronted with just how inauthentic my new dark persona really was. No uniform meant I got to push the limits through fashion. I started wearing women's skinny jeans and crop tops to school and used a Michael Kors purse as my book bag. I needed a way to pad my closet as quickly as possible, so I got a job at my favorite clothing store: Brandy Melville. For those not versed in the religion of UMCWG (upper-middle-class white girls), Brandy Melville is a store where one size fits all, and that size is a double zero with blonde hair and tan skin. We went feral for it. I couldn't believe I got the job, since no other boys worked there, and this toxic environment was a perfect distraction from the hole that theater left.

Final Stop: Find accomplices. Luckily for the bad girl in me, most of my friends were older and could help with my Bad Girl rebrand. Lily, an OG ride or die, and our two other BFFs, Maggie and Brooke, were all baddies already talented in lashing out, as they were a few years older than me. The four of us named our clique the Harlots, and subsequently I changed my Instagram handle to @dylantheharlot. If anyone still questioned my sexuality at that point, my handle definitely solidified my faggotry. My only goal was to implode any and all positive notions my loved ones and the world had previously made about me. That priest made me feel like a villain, and instead of questioning his opinion, I wore my scarlet letter proudly.

The four of us Harlots had HUGE personalities. Yet somehow the other girls were even more dramatic and over the top than me (if you can believe it). Maggie, with her piercing blue eyes and ever-changing hair color, was our ringleader. She was cunning, funny as a whip, and meticulous; she plotted our every move, down to what we'd wear. Sleepovers were often held at Maggie's beachside home, and her mom bankrolled our restaurant sprees and concert tickets. Brooke had the most gorgeous, long blonde hair. She always knew where the party was at, so she was our events coordinator. She is the bluntest person—still to this day—I've ever met. Brooke was the kind of person who seemed to enjoy telling you there was something in your teeth. If you said something ridiculous, she was quick with a "Well, that was fucking stupid." Lily was the oldest and the first of us to drive, so she was our access to the larger world. And Lily was, dare I say, the most gorgeous of us all. I think she sometimes struggled to find true female friendships because women often were intimidated by the attention that she received from men. We were all ex–theater girls in one way or another, but eventually Maggie and Brooke's interests shifted. So, Lily and I would secretly listen to Broadway musicals when it was just us two.

The more we hung out, the more we merged personality traits until we all were the same obnoxious teenager. I did not have main character energy; I was giving gay best friend who always sat in the back of the car energy. I managed to keep up with their antics, like organizing a fake ID order so we could go clubbing, or stealing twenty dollars from my dad's wallet every so often so we could buy something at the mall (sorry, Dad, ily). One of the most out-of-pocket characteristics is that I went from ballet class and show tunes to finding myself in the middle of sweaty mosh pits throwing elbows and screaming along to violent lyrics. Recently, I was surprised to find an Insta post from that era where I quoted the Odd Future lyric "Kill people, burn shit, fuck school."

I felt my authenticity slipping away, but I liked the response my recklessness was getting. My parents were completely distraught over my outbursts, and I gave them little room to advise me. Anytime they would attempt discipline, I would run away to Maggie's house or threaten to never speak to them again.

* * * * *

When we weren't going to parties or driving to rap concerts, the girls and I spent our sleepovers exchanging Chelsea Handler books, desperate to learn about sex. When she came out with her *Chelsea Does* Netflix special, we watched every episode and then watched it all over again. The girls were more sexually experienced than I was, and I didn't want to lose street cred with them, so I added blow jobs to my artillery of weapons. Once I realized that my hookup stories garnered attention with the Harlots, I convinced myself that I wanted to be sexual, even at such a young age.

The problem was that the girls all had guys their own age to hook up with, but there were very few fifteen-year-old out gay boys in my orbit. There were one or two boys in my high school who were openly gay, but we stayed as far away from each other as possible because we didn't want to be grouped together. It's sad, because looking back, it would've been so cool to build a friendship. Since hookups were on my list of Bad Girl Must-Dos, I had to look to older men. I wish I didn't have this instinct, to grow up so fast and give myself so freely. I hated the body I was in, so I didn't see any point in protecting her. I wish I had known at the time how sacred my body, even in that form, was.

The girls supported my experiences with older men because they didn't know better either. We thought we were adults, and that the grown men who wanted to hook up with me just saw me as an equal—mature for my age. I look back at photos of me at this time, and there was nothing mature-looking about me. I was a kid. It sends chills down my spine.

Maggie always said we needed to build an Empire of Men, so that if one of them didn't work out we'd have the next one on speed dial. An Empire of Men. I liked the sound of that. One of my conquests was Rex Coker, who was home from his final year of college, after an internship at *Vogue*. I had drooled over his Facebook profile for years, and I was shocked to see him one night, in the flesh, at a backyard party smoking a cigarette. "Go talk to him!" one of the girls yelled.

"Could I bum a cigarette?" I asked, for the first time in my life.

"Um . . . Yeah," said Rex.

He pulled one out and lit it at my lips. I couldn't believe that a twenty-two-year-old was talking to me, let alone giving me one of his precious cigarettes. I tried to conceal my braces the best I could, never smiling. I breathed in and . . . started coughing uncontrollably.

"Don't inhale so hard," he instructed.

I blushed.

He asked little to nothing about me, and next thing I knew we were in someone's parents' bedroom and I was going down on my Facebook crush (!!!), while trying to be mindful of my braces. I couldn't *wait* to tell the Harlots.

"I'll get you back next time," he said as he zipped up his pants. This wasn't my first time hearing this line—it seemed to be a trend among the masc men I'd been with. The few times it was reciprocated on me back then, I cried because I hated it so much. Whether that was my gender dysphoria, an unwillingness, or both, I can't be sure.

For the rest of the summer, I would indulge Rex whenever he wanted. And because I asked for a cigarette that first night, he assumed I smoked, so I would indulge in a cigarette too. Whatever it took to play with the big kids.

Once Rex left San Diego for New York, he moved on and so did I. I found more gentleman callers, most not age-appropriate. There was one shred of little Dylan's innocence left, and that was my virginity. Somehow, and at the annoyance of my pursuers, I never had full-on sex, at least not until years later in college. I am proud of Dylan the Harlot for waiting until she felt safe and ready.

* * * * *

All of the Harlots graduated high school before me and moved away to figure out life on their own, and eventually I had to follow suit. The characteristics and interests of the other girls quickly dissipated when I looked inward to see that the musical-theater-loving gal still existed within me. I finally left Planet Bad Girl and returned to earth when I saw the light at the end of the tunnel: college. I knew I'd be able to be openly queer in college. Moving away from home meant moving away from all the things that had caused me pain. But in order to get into college, I'd have to put my theater boy costume back on. I pushed the women's clothes to the back of the closet and replaced them with J.Crew polos and khaki pants for auditions. The energy I was putting into being a bad girl now was being rerouted back to the OG goal, Broadway.

* * * * *

Ten years after my Dylan the Harlot chapter and somehow I'm back on Planet Bad Girl. After Beergate, all I want to do is slam my bedroom door in the world's face and scream into my pillow. The song of defiance has returned, and instead of a priest telling me I'm morally corrupt, it's conservative media. It's my DMs. It's the press outside my house. It's the first time I've really craved a cigarette since that summer with Rex Coker. It's as if the past ten years never happened, I am back to hating myself and willing to do anything to show just how much I'm hurting. I'm scared, and queer, and trans, and femme, and depressed. I'd spent a decade learning how to advocate for those parts of myself, and now it's feeling impossible again.

As a child, I had so romanticized the act of growing up, the littlest adult. Now I've made it here and it's not at all how I imagined. I lie in bed wishing away this reality. I had just gotten to a place where my transness didn't feel like a curse, and now it feels like a death sentence. If not at the hand of a crazy extremist, then by my own. When Dylan the Harlot was struggling, at least she knew that adulthood held endless possibilities if reached. I sit here in adulthood looking forward, but the mess feels too big and the possibilities feel too complicated. Like seeing the pile of clothes on your bed and being too tired and overwhelmed to tidy them up, so you decide to just sleep on top of them.

I wonder if my followers can see my hurt. I don't want to burden them, so I put on a fake smile or don't post at all. I'll upload little cries for help and swiftly delete them minutes later. But just when I thought that I had sealed my fate of perpetual pain, Dylan the Harlot sent me a Hail Mary.

DAY 107 of being a girl . . .

. . . And I tried a tomato. I HATED IT.

I'm at a health retreat in Northern California with
Keesh. After day 100, I knew I was gonna need a major
reboot, and Keesh recommended we both visit her favorite
woo-woo retreat in the woods to decompress and unpack
the insanity of the past three months. I was a bit
worried that it would take longer than a week to rid
myself of all the Domino's and Advil PMs I've ingested
over the years, but happy to take a crack at it. I traded

consuming content for vegetables, took off the fake lashes, and dusted off my Birkenstocks. It's only a week. I can do a week! Besides, after all the shaving I've done and all the makeup I've had to cake on every day, this was a good opportunity to give my skin some rest.

Before *Days of Girlhood*, I regularly dabbled in all things woo-woo.

Dylan's Woo-Woo Starter Kit

- Biannual psychic visits

- A quarterly yoga class

- A Yosemite National Park obsession

- Shrooms at the hot springs

- One muumuu, preferably tie-dye and cat-themed

- At least one pair of hiking boots

Upon arrival, I was hesitant to let my guard down with the two female practitioners leading the retreat, Satya and Ama, even though it was just the four of us for the week. Would they see my addiction to content creation as trivial and below them? Or, worse, what if they landed on the TERF side of the tracks? I'd assume woo-woo women in the woods would be accepting, but after the scrutiny I've faced online, I fear that judgment can lurk around any corner. But Keesh has been coming here for years, and I feel safe enough to give it a try.

We were instructed to tell Satya what we wanted to fix in our lives so that she could create tailored treatments. Satya is one of these long-haired ladies who very much seems like the kind of goddess who was born under a full moon during a birthing ritual. Keesh's intention was to get rid of a rash, and my intention was to detox from TikTok. Most of my regimen involved being separated from my phone, eating healthy food, having practitioners give me energy treatments, and meditating. I also did a treatment where a practitioner dropped a steady stream of oil on my head to open up my third eye. It was woo-woo waterboarding.

We also could only consume coffee by doing an enema, and while I'm not sure how drinking coffee through my bootyhole would cure a TikTok addiction . . . at least I was properly prepped for any backdoor play I might find in the woods. Another thing they had me do was chug a large cup of olive oil before bed to flush out my liver and gallbladder, in the hopes that I'd get rid of gallstones in the morning. Not only did I not produce any stones, I had the most unrestful night of my life. It's kind of hard to fall asleep when you're on the brink of throwing up, so I just dramatically writhed around the bed. I didn't have Netflix or even a podcast to lull me back to sleep because these enlightened, long-haired guardians took their jobs very seriously and confiscated my devices.

The morning after my sleepless night, Keesh and I convinced Satya to let us go into town for a few hours to show me Nevada City, an old mining town nearby. I even managed to get my phone back after smartly pointing out we needed the GPS to navigate into town. I wore Keesh's vintage Princess Diana T-shirt and cowboy boots to lean into the Western vibe. I love a theme.

A Conversation with Keesh in the Car

Me: I WANT A PICKLE!

Keesh: You can't eat a pickle. It will completely ruin the diet they have us on.

Me: But it's a vegetable!!!

Keesh: There's so much salt, though.

Me: I DON'T CARE! IT'S A MIRACLE I'VE MADE IT THIS FAR.

Keesh convinced me to wait until we went to the grocery store at the end of the day. Keesh thought that if I could wait that long, then maybe I'd realize I wouldn't need to mess up our detox with vinegar and salt. I knew I'd buckle either way, so I agreed to wait. We walked around the country town, popping into tourist boutiques I would never normally shop at, but after days of isolation they felt like Nordstrom. Everything looked like it was made from a cow down the street.

As I was walking out of a store, a little boy handed me a pink Starburst and told me it was for Kindness Day. I wanted to tell him it was the cruelest thing he'd ever done but said "thank you" instead.

"Don't do it," Keesh urged, seeing the glimmer in my eye.

"You know pink is my favorite fruit," I whined.

"You'll get sick, it'll be no fun."

I put the Starburst in my pocket and took a moment to be wildly impressed by my willpower.

Keesh and I did a photoshoot in a saloon, took mirror selfies, and I got my reward at the grocery store, a dill pickle, for Dyl pickle. After days of unsweetened oatmeal and lentil broth, that pickle was the best-tasting thing I'd ever had in my life.

I took the drive back as an opportunity to pop into my Instagram, and I was semi-surprised to see my follower

count hadn't dropped to zero in my absence. I had zero
guilt about breaking my phone fast. Considering how
addicted I am, it's a miracle I'd gone three days without
my fix of *Twilight* memes, animal videos, and voice memos
to Lily. I deserved my pickle and Instagram scroll!

When I got back to the lodge, I was tempted to post a
video but knew there was no way I'd be given that much
alone time with my phone, so I settled for a mirror
selfie to my story instead. Phone off and back in the
hands of Satya.

Now came the hardest task of all during the week:
three days of silence. I can't think of anything
worse than being quiet. I would love for someone
to count how many words I say in a day. Actually,

scratch that, how many seconds of silence there are in my days. I say seconds, because not a minute goes by where I'm not shooting the shit. Even alone, I am talking to myself constantly. Talking to yourself was ALSO against the rules for our silence period, which was the worst part. WAIT! I know what's even worse! Having my beloved friend right next to me, the friend I get to see so rarely and have so much to fill her in on, and I CAN'T SAY SHIT TO HER! Phoneless, no chatting, sucking coffee up the butt, and gulping down olive oil. Welcome to my version of hell, ladies.

* * * * *

I learned a lot about myself during these three days—specifically that I am constantly seeking affirmation from those around me. But without the ability to ask for validation, I had to provide it for myself . . . with my MIND. I was itching to acknowledge the weather, the food, the feeling of the day with the people around me. Anything! I hated all the silence almost as much as I hated that tomato I was forced to try.

I journaled a lot. I found worth in this pause. I learned that distance from my phone wasn't going to kill me and my career, that it's okay to be silent around close friends, and that I'm still capable of finding peace. But during a weak moment, while Satya was cooking dinner and not paying attention, I had an opportunity to grab my phone and all that learning went out the window. When I turned it on, I found that I had NINE missed calls from my entertainment lawyer. Huh?

"Hi, Dylan, the not-Apple-smartphone team is in a tizzy over your Instagram selfie using an iPhone when you are still under contract with *their* phone, including not being photographed with anything but their smartphone. I know you're out of town, but if you could please call me so this doesn't escalate, I'd appreciate it."

"FUCKKKKKKK!" I screamed . . . but in my head, because I wasn't allowed to talk. I had managed to avoid the social media world for almost the entire week, and the one time I chose to engage I voided my biggest brand contract to date. This must be karma for eating that pickle.

I was spiraling. Are they going to sue me?! Am I done for?!!!! I went to dial my lawyer and paused. *Am I about to break my silence for this?*

Hell yes, I am.

I was having no luck getting service in the house, so I started running through the trees trying to catch bars, until I hit the pond. I finally got through. "I AM SO SORRY," I huffed out.

"It's fine. Too late to delete the story."

"Please tell them I will do anything. I'll post
their phone to my story over and over."

"I'll let them know. Try and go enjoy
the rest of your trip."

I hung up and saw Satya and Keesh looking out at me
on the deck. They obviously heard me break my
vow of silence. I mouthed, "AN EMERGENCY."
Seeing Satya's face, though, I became more
afraid of breaking her rules than a potential
lawsuit. These woo-woo gals mean business.

When we broke silence that night, I reenacted the
drama of the day, fully committing to every movement
and detail of the smartphone saga. Being able to share
the absurdity of the mistake I'd made, and get a laugh
for it, felt good. It solidified that taking trauma and
turning it into comedy is my specialty. Hearing the
ladies' laughter gave me that same little high that
performing does. It was now evident that no matter my
facial hair or my following, these three women honored
the woo-woo woman that's always been inside me. Satya's
motherly care and passion made me gain a deep level of
respect for the work that we had done over the week.

Today is our last day of the retreat, and I feel
somewhat ready to return to my online life. To
celebrate, I shaved my full beard in the morning and
put a little makeup on. Overall, this TikTok detox was
worth it. It's a good reminder to invest in myself, even

if it means I have to chug a cup of oil every now and then. I'm sad to leave Keesh, but I know I'll see her for our annual Christmas trip to the hot springs. All in all, seems like this week fixed EVERYTHING. Back to being a *well-oiled* content-making machine, baby.

LOVE YA,

Dylan♥

P.S. I still have that pink Starburst sitting, unwrapped, at my house as a sweet little reminder of my willpower.

DAY 135 of being a girl . . .

. . . And Houston, we *do not* have lift off. I've been so
busy these last few months that I haven't had the free
time to explore my sexual pleasures, both personal
and with others. By the time I finish editing videos
and answering emails, the only thing happening in
my canopy bed is Domino's and sleep. What I hadn't
realized, or possibly hadn't wanted to confront, was the
fact that my sex drive was slowly but surely dwindling. I
knew this was a normal side effect of the hormones, and
I was so happy with the results of them otherwise. Low
sex drive seemed like a fair trade-off. But last night,
there was . . . nothing. It was drier than the cinnamon
challenge. Funny enough, it reminded me of the first
time I orgasmed as a teen—I was so scared of what
happened to my body that I asked Google, "Am I dying?"

This time I knew I wasn't dying, but if I were to
never orgasm ever again, I'd grieve for sure. The
only thing I can compare it to is watching the iconic
song "Defying Gravity" from *Wicked,* where Elphaba
the witch is supposed to soar over the stage in a
major climax, but just as the music builds and the
band swells, the actress's harness malfunctions
and you're left with a flightless witch. You are still

seeing a musical, but there's no Broadway magic. At least I was seeing a show, right? Well, not for long.

A little background into my sex life: I have yet to be kissed as a girl, but I had my fair share of kisses as a boy back in the day. None of which were spectacular in any way. BUT DON'T FRET! Transitioning feels like a do-over! I'm so ready to get scooped up in someone's arms while we watch *Twilight* and rub on each other.

(I'm team Edward by the way, but recently have become attracted to Kristen Stewart, so I guess I'm Team Bella too. That might be my dream threesome? Totally.)

Come to think of it, I may prefer watching movies and spooning to actual full-on sex, and that might be good now that Missy is not operating at full capacity.

Missy was the name of my first car, a white Volkswagen Passat, and also what we're going to use to refer to my penis. Missy (the car) was so unpredictable and broke down constantly, I never named a car ever again. Feels fitting.

P.S. Girl, we are NOT talking about this on TikTok, okay?! Fox News would have a field day.

I can already see the headline now: "Grown man parading as 'Audrey Hepburn Reincarnated' Faces the Consequences by Lack of Boner." And what a news segment that would be.

I've always had a complicated relationship with Missy. Technically she's done nothing wrong, it's not her fault that she goes out instead of in. Still, sometimes I wish it was just a smooth piece of skin with no orifice in sight like Barbie. It would be difficult to pee, but at least I wouldn't feel so conflicted about the future of my crotch. Bottom surgery is still so far away for me, if I choose to pursue it, and I'm all about one step at a time. Facial feminization surgery is my top priority at the moment, because when I look in the mirror, I do not see the person I was born to be, and there's very little I can do to conceal that. But down there, I can get creative (I'm looking at you, tucking tape). The one thing I know is that if I do get bottom surgery, it will be because *I* want it. Part of me thinks I would proudly share the news of getting a vagina, to shut at least some of the haters up, but I also want to hold value in the fact that trans women don't need bottom surgery to be acceptable versions of transness. I've shared everything else so publicly, I hope my followers can respect my privacy on that one.

I froze my sperm at the beginning of transition, so I could keep all my reproductive options open, but I wish I would've at least hooked up with SOMEONE while I had the full ability to. Or maybe it's better that I didn't because they would fall in love with Missy and then they too would have to say goodbye. This is all making me a little down. I'm going to put my sexual woes aside and cheer myself up with some musical theater.

* * * * *

Tonight I went to the Hollywood Bowl to meet up with a new friend, and it was immaculate timing, because my trans gal pal had plenty to say on the topic. During intermission, I told her about my inability to get hard, and she really turned my perspective upside down.

A Conversation During *Kinky Boots* Intermission

Her: Isn't it the best?

Wait, wha? I was confused. This is a good thing?

Me: Uh, I'm not sure yet.

Her: Getting my Cassie was the best thing I ever did.

First Missy, and now CASSIE?! This is getting out of hand!

Me: Who's Cassie?

Her: Cassie is what we call castration. I got my balls chopped off. Now it just flops around. But if that's not your cup of tea, sounds like you need a slight hormone adjustment.

NEW SCENARIO HAS ENTERED THE CHAT. You're telling me there's an option between bottom surgery and keeping it? Woah. I don't know if Cassie is right for Missy, but at least we know about her now. And I made a new trans gal pal who I feel like I can trust.

"Good night, Missy!"

"Good night, Cassie!"

Good night, Dylan.

LOVE YA,

Dylan ♥

Chapter 5

A(N AYAHUASCA)
TRIP TO PERU

I think most trans people have strongly ingrained survival tactics. My survival tactic has always been to look for the light. That light at the end of the tunnel has always saved me from my dark thoughts and suicidal ideation. When I was a small trans kid, the light at the end of the tunnel was my queerness. During high school it was college, in college it was Broadway. I have a tendency to hyperfixate on an external event in the future that will be the cure to all my sadness, heartbreak, and loneliness. As Beergate continued at an unrelenting pace, the light grew dimmer and the cure-all did not present itself. Little did I know that @dylantheharlot would be the one reflecting it back to me.

One afternoon, I was looking at the next month's calendar only to see next to nothing on the books. Flipping back to last year's calendar, my July was filled from morning to evening every single day. The only concrete plan I had was to attend Mikayla Nogueira's wedding on July 1 in Newport, Rhode Island. As I was looking into flights, I got a Marco Polo video from the one and only Chelsea Handler, who I became close with after guesting on her podcast. Marco Polo is a slightly archaic app, and I use it exclusively to message with Chelsea, because we found we're incompatible without it. I hate texting and she hates phone calls, so this way we send video walkie-talkie messages back and forth. As I watched her latest message showing me her swanky hotel room, my @dylantheharlot self smiled. I was quickly reminded of my obsession with Chelsea's Netflix docuseries *Chelsea Does*.

In her *Chelsea Does Drugs* episode, she travels to Peru to try ayahuasca, one of the strongest drugs in the world. I remember watching and thinking, *Well, I'm gonna do THAT one day.* Taking ayahuasca isn't something to be done lightly, so if I was going to participate, I needed to treat it like the sacred practice that it is. They say you'll know when it's the right time to try ayahuasca because you're called to it, and on this late June day, Chelsea's Marco Polo still playing in my hands, ayahuasca called to me.

I was ready to hop on a plane to Peru that very second if it meant I wouldn't be sad anymore. I immediately looked up retreats, and I found that most were groups of ten to twelve strangers taking it together for a week in the jungle. I don't feel called to throwing up in a bucket in front of anyone who might film it and send it to Fox News, so a group retreat felt out of the question. I'd need to ask for help, so I called my agent, who once told me of a friend who moved down to Peru to start an ayahuasca center.

That very day, I was on the phone with Alyssa, an ex–music agent who tried ayahuasca a few years ago and loved it so much that she moved to Peru. Wait, moved there?! This made me nervous I too might leave my life in Hollywood to live in the mountains of Peru. I wanted the ayahuasca to help me navigate this wild lifestyle, not drive me away from it entirely. After relocating, Alyssa teamed up with a shaman to start private retreats for anyone looking to take their own ayahuasca journey. And she was very gracious, answering the millions of questions I'd sent her at all hours of the day. Questions like: Will my Dyson Airwrap work down there? If anything were to go wrong, what is the emergency care like? Can I pet an alpaca? Do they have Trader Joe's or something comparable? At a certain point, I stopped asking questions and surrendered to the uncertainty. I was desperate to see the light. "Throw-up bucket, party of one?! SIGN ME UP!"

As soon as I bought the flight, it was game on. First, Alyssa instructed, I'd need to start a dieta immediately. A dieta is the detox that takes place before taking ayahuasca. This meant no processed foods, no sugar, no medications, no caffeine, and no sex for weeks beforehand. I also would have to go off my hormones, which probably would concern my doctor, while I was mostly concerned about losing the cleavage momentum I'd recently gained. The sex would be no issue for me (see Day 135), but cutting out my main source of nutrients—junk food—was nearly a deal-breaker. When I told Alyssa this, she said she'd allow a little bit of whole-grain bread here and there—a mini light at the end of the tunnel.

Before embarking on this intense trip, I knew there was one thing I needed to let go of, and it was the bowling ball of anxiety sitting on my chest. Ever since Beergate, I knew the right thing to do was speak out and be honest about what had happened, but the important figures in my life urged me not to. Still, I felt uneasy. People were buying beer to support me, but they didn't know how bad things were behind the scenes. I tried for three months to let the desire to share my side fade, but I knew I was in a moment when the world needed honesty, and I owed it to the trans community and my followers.

I had decided the best course of action was to do what I do best: make a video. I planned to tell everyone what transpired through this brand deal and issue a call to action for allies to show up for us when we need it most. I thought about waiting until after ayahuasca to make the video, but I knew the bowling ball on my chest would only grow bigger and potentially ruin any sort of healing that could happen down in Peru. So, on June 30, the last day of Pride Month, I once again hit record. I posted the video as I was leaving for the airport, the bowling ball starting to shrink.

I flew from LA to Newport, Rhode Island, for Mikayla's wedding, where I watched beauty influencers and other guests down champagne, desserts, and a whole menu of items that were not on the dieta. I went into a sugar withdrawal. Luckily, my date, Chris Olsen, was sober, so the desire to get blackout drunk wasn't there. During the toasts, I dug into my mac and cheese and looked up only to see Chris giving me a funny stare. "Are you sure you're allowed to eat that during your detox?" he asked me. "Oh, honey," I told him, "if it isn't out the microwave, it's healthy for me." The mac and cheese made me feel a bubble of joy, or maybe that was just the few sips of champagne I did sneak at the reception.

* * * * *

PART I

On the plane to Peru, I started wondering if the thing that was going to fix my mental health, ayahuasca, could be the thing to make it a hundred times worse. What if I wasn't ready to process trauma at this high a level? Especially when so much of it was still so fresh? My video exposé was responded to very positively, and people couldn't believe what had really gone down. My chest was a thousand times lighter. But what was now sitting in the bowling ball's place was the water balloon of fear that I might be sued for airing out dirty laundry. While I did my best to not commit defamation or disparagement, I couldn't guarantee that my video would go over well with Beergate execs. I played it out in my head, and decided that if I were to be sued, at least I stood up for something and I went down swinging. Plus, I think my court outfits would be ICONIC. If a lawyer man knocks on the shaman's yurt to serve me papers, so be it.

Since my only frames of reference for Peru were the Chelsea Drug Doc and the *Emperor's New Groove* movie, I really had no idea what to expect. When I arrived in Cusco, I was greeted by cool weather and dry air, not the jungle that Chelsea went to on her show. Alyssa picked me up from the airport holding a mango smoothie. Mangos? Something very out of my wheelhouse. I tried my best to suck it down, despite the pulp, and smiled through the discomfort.

After an hour of driving, Alyssa made up for the pulp-y mango smoothie tenfold by bringing me to an animal sanctuary. She remembered that right behind enlightenments, my second goal of this trip was to pet alpacas. Llamas, check! Alpacas, check! Some weird birds, check! Now all that was left to check off my list was enlightenment.

We pulled up to a housing commune, where a handsome Spanish man in his sixties greeted us at the gate. He owned the small community and showed me to the house I'd have all to myself. It was four bedrooms, slightly bougie, and ICE COLD. I didn't realize that Peru was in their winter, and I did *not* pack appropriately. My frozen fingers shuffled through my sports bras and biker shorts, looking for a good aya outfit. I walked down to the maloca, a one-room yurt in the middle of the property, where I would be taking the ayahuasca.

Alyssa, who was sitting right outside the entrance of the yurt, popped up from her crisscross applesauce and invited me in.

"This is Onanya,* your guide for the journey ahead," she said. Onanya was a little over five feet tall, wearing traditional Peruvian textiles, and had a smile that instantly made me feel like everything was going to be alright. He bowed his head, so I did the same. "Onanya doesn't speak English and I speak some Spanish, but we can use Google translate if we need." Uh-oh.

We began with a meditation that included an energy clearing by smoking tobacco. They passed me the hand-rolled cigarette, reminiscent of a blunt, and I laughed. Back in the States, I was smacking my wrist over the grossness of the few half-cigarettes that I had smoked, and now here I am being encouraged to smoke for my health. Funny how the things we run from find us. I guess it's all a frame of mind.

I was excused for the evening and told to return around 8 p.m. for the first ceremony, which was when the drinking of the ayahuasca would take place. In the meantime, I was supposed to write my

---

* I'm using Onanya as the name of my healer to protect his privacy. Onanya is a word from the Shipibo-Conibo language meaning "a person who has wisdom."

intentions of what I wanted to accomplish while on this journey. Oh, and take a plant bath with a bucket of leaves Onanya had handed me. I'd never taken a plant bath with a bucket of leaves before, so I asked for clear instructions. "At the very end of the shower," Alyssa told me, "dump the leaves all over your body and try not to wash it off too much." Lily called on FaceTime right as I was about to pour the sacred plant bath, and I answered. "I'm taking a plant bath, can you please be reverent for a second while I do this."

The water from the shower was nowhere near hot, so I shivered in the tub until I gave up and finally dumped the plants over my head. I swear to God I had sacred foliage in all my crevices, but I took it seriously and let them stick to my body. "I'm a walking salad," I said through chattering teeth to Lily. Instead of making a joke back, Lily went quiet. She was really nervous for me because she was paranoid it could go poorly. Before getting off the phone, I assured her I was ready for this experience. That I needed it, whatever it was. I put on my warmest, coziest clothes, including my tie-dye cat muumuu, and took out my journal to begin writing down my intentions.

A little before 8 p.m., I walked down in my pink Crocs in the dark of night, careful not to step on any horse poo-poo—there was a rogue horse walking about, which made me a little nervous. A horse bit me when I was young, so you can imagine how I . . . okay, this is irrelevant, sorry, let's stay focused. I approached the maloca with the excitement of a kid about to shake their Christmas presents. Was I fully prepared to participate in this Indigenous practice? What will I find, and will I like it? What if I don't? Would I miss the bucket and puke on myself? Onanya was already playing music on a flute and Alyssa was on a yoga mat a few feet from the cot I was to lie on for my trip.

The circular wooden structure had no lights except for the giant full moon shining down from the skylight above. I wondered if it was actually full. Would need to Google that when I get back to my room, along with how to say *emergency* in Spanish. It was cold in this yurt too, and I kept asking for more blankets until I felt like I had a linebacker lying on top of me. That's better. I watched as Onanya took out the ayahuasca from his bag, which was in a plastic water bottle, and poured it into a small clay jug.

"We bought this today since we thought it looked a little more special than just taking it from the water bottle," chimed Alyssa. Onanya poured me a cup, and it came out slow like brown sludge molasses. A thick shot. My limited palate would've gladly had ten pulpy mango smoothies in comparison. Alyssa translated that I would start with one cup, and then as the night went on, I could ask for another if I felt called. The ayahuasca itself tasted like cooked grass with dirt and cough syrup buried under a witch's house for three thousand years and then dug out and slopped straight into my cup. Technically speaking, I believe it's boiled water using special combinations of vines from the jungle, but I'm not one to ask too many questions when it comes to what I'm ingesting.

I choked it down as I shuffled through the many intentions I wanted to target. It reminded me of every birthday I've had, thinking through a dozen different wishes while blowing out the candles. Those wishes don't usually come true, so I thought for this journey, it'd be better to settle on one: I want to know where I came from. The more I become myself, the less I understand about how I got here in the first place. I am interested to know if there was anything before this life.

I settled into my cot and waited for the magic to come. I stared at the moon, growing anxious as time passed with not so much as a buzz. After what felt like ages, I asked how long it would take, and Alyssa said an hour, which it definitely had been. I tried to stay in a sacred state of mind, but my thoughts kept drifting back to LA. "Will I ever get another brand deal?" "Why didn't I get invited to the *Barbie* premiere?" *No, no turn those off, Dylan, those are impure influencer thoughts.* I started to think that ayahuasca might not work for me—DAMMIT I shouldn't have had that wedding mac and cheese. Did I not go off my hormones for long enough? Maybe ayahuasca and I just weren't compatible and I'm in Peru and I already saw alpacas and there's nothing left.

Just as my spiral was hitting something darker, I saw it: a black-and-white palm tree. And then another. And another. There were infinite geometric colorless palm fronds behind my eyelids, and I was scared that if I opened my eyes they would be gone and I wouldn't know how to see them again. I put the blankets over my head and opened my eyes. The palms were still there. I closed my eyes again. The geometric shapes were growing larger and stronger. I smiled. The mac and cheese didn't stop me from finding something.

* * * * *

The shapes I was seeing faded away, until I saw the purest pitch black, different from what I usually see when I close my eyes. Slowly, new shapes appeared, and these new shapes were in the most vibrant shades. Colors I could only describe as electric. I saw trees, pyramids, animals, and patterns. Most notably, a bright yellow jaguar walked alongside me for quite some time. The only thing on earth that I could compare these visuals to were the graphics on the slot machines that my mom plays. Bright, bold, warm, welcoming, addictive. But even that doesn't really do justice to their extraordinary beauty. I knew I had traveled somewhere in my mind that was nowhere near earth. The colorful shapes became less and less defined until I was coasting through billions of pastel dots speeding by me. It wasn't the first time I was there; in my heart I knew this is where I came from. Finally, after traveling millions of miles away from this cot, I was placed down on a pink glowing lotus-type flower, a sort of amoeba. The only thing on earth that feels even remotely close to comparison is the monster from *Nope*. But this was no monster. I knew this was Mother Ayahuasca.

Onanya and Alyssa had told me that Mother Ayahuasca often appears or makes herself known to those who partake, but I had no idea she would feel this tangible, this heavenly. As I lay with her, my eyes began running with tears. I'd been waiting for this reunion. I'd never felt that safe in my human life. The joy I felt hiding under my comforter in bed for hours at a time couldn't hold a candle to this ecstasy. I never wanted to leave.

Right then, I felt myself being pulled away from Mother Aya, and the color faded, until I was ejected into cold black-and-white, sharp lines. Pain like I'd never experienced seared through me. Immediately, I knew it was my human birth that happened years and years ago.

I was mad at Mother Aya for bringing me back to my earth life, and I was resentful of my new surroundings. But she told me I decided to come here by my choice.

"That's hard to believe," I scoffed. She simply laughed.

I tried to distract myself from this new pain by examining my purpose—maybe discovering what it was that could make the hurt worth it. I racked my brain for possibilities; I thought about the joy I felt being onstage making people smile, I thought about the DMs from queer teens saying that I'd helped them come out. Maybe I'd already found it? But Mother Aya just laughed again and said, "Nothing you've done so far is what your bigger purpose is."

I wrinkled my nose, almost offended. You're telling me all the trauma I've been through amounts to nothing? "No," she responded, "you're here to be a mother."

"A mother?" I asked her. I've always kept the possibility of having children open for the future, but as I've become more and more polarizing in the media, motherhood felt like less and less of an option.

"Yes, you are here to be a mom. To your children and also to the queer young people of the world who don't have the love they need to thrive." I sat with this and thought about what it would mean to raise children in this world as a trans woman. Not to mention the scrutiny my children would face by simply being associated with me. I would never want to subject a child to humiliation or shame. But then she showed me what motherhood could look like, and that worry melted away. As I held two babies in my arms, I cried, because I hadn't let myself envision this future out of fear. Whether that's in the cards for me or not, it was a sweet release into a life I didn't think possible.

And here's where shit gets realllllly weird. How do I put this . . . I lactated out of my nipples.

Now, you might be thinking, Dylan, you metaphorically lactated, right? I thought the same thing, at first. Until I felt the shirt on my body starting to become soaked, not with sweat. I opened my eyes, looked down, and sure enough, my nipples were LEAKING. I got scared.

"Um, Alyssa?"

"Is everything okay?" she asked.

"I, um, think that liquid is coming out of my nipples. Is that normal?"

I heard her whisper something to Onanya before telling me, "Yup, he says everything is fine, and to go back in."

I settled in, being transported back within seconds, and had a few pressing questions.

"In this moment, I feel so loved," I told Mother Aya, "but what about all those people who despise me so much? How can you make me feel so valuable but send me into a world where they see me as repulsive? What's the deal with Ted Cruz?" I might be the first person to acknowledge Ted Cruz's existence while tripping on ayahuasca.

"Those people lack a mother's love. They only understand the conditional," she told me. "Show them what unconditional love looks like."

There it was. *My purpose.* I smiled. Just as this peace started to stick, I felt my gurgling stomach make some bigger moves—upward and outward. I projectile vomited into the bucket provided. I'm not a fan of throwing up, but it felt like I was releasing twenty-six years of gunk, emotional and physical. (I've swallowed a lot of gum in my day, and that for sure came out.)

After I had vomited out what I thought was the last bit, a dark powder came shooting out of my mouth and into the bucket. It was a little startling but oh so satisfying. I felt the dimension I had visited start to fade around me until I was confident I could pull off a decent parallel park job, indicating to me that I was nearly sober. I lifted up my stack of blankets and peered up at the moon above me. This time, it looked so much clearer. No Google needed; I knew it was full. Alyssa must have fallen asleep, because when I began rustling, she took a spooked breath. "You doing okay?" she asked.

"Um . . . I think so? I'm . . . really hungry," I replied. She asked Onanya if I was allowed a snack, and he said yes. Thank God. She left for the kitchen and returned with a single slice of whole wheat bread. Jackpot.

I waddled back to the house, my Crocs squishing into the ground after assuring Alyssa and Onanya that I was totally fine to get back alone; I wasn't quite ready to talk to anyone and I needed to process. I took tiny bites of the slice of bread as I dodged horse poo-poo.

Back at my place, I twiddled my thumbs, not sure of what to do. In a lot of ways, I had never felt more sober. I was scared. How was I supposed to go back to normal life making TikToks and online shopping after I had just seen what I now believe to be heaven? Shit, am I going to pull an Alyssa and move here full-time?

Sitting in that cold room, I began to feel like Mother Ayahuasca was so much more tangible than God. Like I had proof of her existence. As soon as I began thinking this, my Catholicism instantly kicked in. "Don't worship false idols," a small voice warned. Not sure how else to process, I decided to journal every detail that night so I wouldn't forget a thing. Once I was done, I went back to twiddling my thumbs. Now what? Do I masturbate? That's not on the dieta menu, so it's off the table. I just wanted to do something that felt human, that could ground me back to this life that I had supposedly chosen. I opened my laptop and put on the most human thing of all: the pilot episode of *Gilmore Girls*. As Rory and Lorelai rattled through pop culture reference after pop culture reference at the speed of light, I drifted off to sleep.

* * * * *

The next day, I woke up only to realize it was the Fourth of July. Lol. Celebrating the Fourth of July by doing ancient hallucinogens in South America is not how I thought things would go! Feeling hungry, I raced down to the maloca for what I hoped would be more slices of bread for breakfast. I should have slept in, because what was waiting for me was fruit. And oatmeal.

"We don't want to overwhelm your body with carbs after such a heavy trip. Plus, you're doing another ceremony tonight," Alyssa explained.

I fought the urge to tell her that the fruit was what *would* overwhelm my body, but instead, I just smiled and tried to eat around the parts of the oatmeal that were touched by nature's chunky accessories. Then Alyssa's words really sunk in. I'm doing this all over again TONIGHT?! I forgot that I had agreed to four ceremonies that week. Damn. Last night would be a tough act to follow. After I choked down my breakfast, I was instructed to journal, meditate, and rest before another go of it.

Back in my room, more than anything I wanted to continue with *Gilmore Girls*, but I knew that probably was not the best use of my time. That's the funny part of adulthood—you can finally do whatever you want but still feel the nagging voice in your head. "Get your money's worth!" I could hear my dad clearly. I doubt he'd be saying that about doing psychedelics, though. Luckily, I kept my life coaching appointment with Mory that day, and she was the perfect person to unpack the night before with. While on the call with Mory, we made a plan for my next three trips: 1. How to integrate this new knowledge into the real world; 2. Healing my inner child and old trauma; and 3. How to approach my future self and manifestation. I love an itinerary.

* * * * *

PART II

When it was time for my second journey, I walked down to the maloca with a swagger in my step. I was no longer scared of uncharted territory; I knew what to expect from the ayahuasca and I also knew where the horse poo-poo was located. Alyssa and Onanya were waiting for me, and I took my spot under the stack of blankets on my cot. This time, I wore every single piece of clothing I brought to stay warm. Onanya brought over the thick thick, and I knew what taste was in store. I winced before the cup even touched my lips. The gagging was worth what was to come; I couldn't wait to see Mother Aya again. The silent hour before liftoff wasn't as frustrating as the previous night's. Before I knew it, I was back to seeing the black-and-white geometric palms, as if they were a "You've Made It to Heaven, Population You!" sign. I could feel myself in limbo, calling out to Mother Aya, waiting for her presence. But she wasn't showing up, so I was left sorting shapes and colors by myself. I grew annoyed. Then the judgmental thoughts came in. "She showed me all of that last night and now doesn't have time for me. I came all this way. I drank the thick thick. Maybe it's just a one-time experience." After a while of childish agonizing, I finally heard her. This time, she wasn't a yummy pink lotus flower, she was a voice in the particles of light whizzing around me.

"Guilt will never work," she said. Now I really felt her. She was not stern, but not soft at the moment either. "The more you try to force something, the less it will grow," she told me.

My classic guilt trip tactics that work on earth were not going to make a dent in this mama. I was now the one who felt guilty, not just from trying it with her, but all of the guilt I've put onto other relationships during my lifetime. I thought about how often I put my mom in the doghouse. She's in a constant state of trying to gain back my trust. I thought about the ultimatums I put onto her, especially as a teen. "If you don't accept me right now in this second, you aren't my mom anymore," I told her in that therapist's office at fourteen. I constantly threatened to take away her title. "You need to forgive her," Mother Aya told me, knowing exactly where my mind was. Is it that easy? I thought about Dana back in San Diego right at that moment, probably scrolling on her iPad with *American Pickers* on in the background. I missed her. I remembered that I was once growing in her and that she probably was in cahoots with Mother Aya to bring me here to this earth, whether she knew it or not.

This line of thinking must have been enough for Mother Aya to take me to my next scene. Suddenly, I was back in the bed where I lost my virginity at nineteen. My trips thus far were mostly mental and not physical (aside from the lactation), but now my body felt tense. Quickly, I flickered through all the men I had let inside me. I was confronted with the desire and willingness on my part and the lack of care and love from my partners. "Your body is a vessel, and when you let someone in, there needs to be an equal exchange of energy," she told me through my tears. After each man faded away, I felt little pieces of myself chipping off like porcelain. Though I knew I was on a cot in Peru, my body felt like it was being used over and over again. Once I reached the last person I was with, I was like, "Jesus, Mother Aya, at least buy me dinner first." Afterward, I felt empty. But Mother Aya assured me that there would be plenty of opportunities for equal love exchange, ones that wouldn't leave me feeling like shattered porcelain.

This was the first time I was glad that I hadn't had sex in years. I subconsciously knew that it was hurting me. The more I tried to fuck away my feelings, the further away from actual, good love I got.

I was getting very, very sweaty at this point, and then came the vomit. Not refreshing like the night before's experience. This was full-on "I had expired milk and I'm calling in sick to work" type puke. My bones hurt as they tried to hold me together while I was convulsing. And then the high was over.

"Can I have my bread now?" I moaned. Alyssa returned from the kitchen with not one, but two pieces this time.

"Since there are no ceremonies tomorrow, you can indulge a bit," she said as she handed over the bread. I was thrilled. Some more journaling. One more episode of *Gilmore Girls*. Another night's journey not to be believed.

No ayahuasca ceremony the next night meant I could finally eat a full meal. Alyssa was willing to prepare fish, but I had learned (googled) that the surrounding town had a few five-star resorts, which I drooled over after my ice-cold showers. "Can I take you to dinner at the fancy resort?" I asked her, putting on my sweetest tone. "Oh . . . well . . . we'll have to be careful about what you order. And we need to invite Onanya too." So Alyssa, Onanya, and I put on our nicest sweatshirts for the Tambo del Inka Marriott property.

"Order whatever you want!" I exclaimed as I read through the menu, salivating over every item covered in cheese. I also convinced Alyssa and Onanya that we should order booze because it was a special occasion. "What's the occasion?" Alyssa asked. "It's a Wednesday and I'm in Peru!!!" I laughed. She refused to let me order my own but let me celebrate by having a few sips of her pisco sour, a traditional Peruvian drink. Yum. We tried to use Google translate to make jokes with Onanya, and the nonsensical translations paired with the language barrier had all three of us laughing. Alyssa told me about Onanya's family, who lives in the jungle and has been conducting ayahuasca ceremonies for generations. Together, they hope to get a business going with the hopes of expanding into the States. Even though I think everyone should have access to healing ceremonies, I'm still glad I came down to Peru for the full experience (and not a white guy's backyard in Malibu). That night, I happily fell asleep, with a belly full of cheese.

* * * * *

PART III

Third night's the charm, right? Oh, bitch. I settled into my cot thinking I knew it all. I went in with the intention Mory and I had talked about earlier in the week, trying to heal my inner child of her trauma. I might have intentioned too close to the sun. Right after the black-and-white palms, I saw myself as a small kid, seven years old being hot-boxed in my babysitter's car; Bethany was smoking weed while I was holding my breath.

Once again, I was scrooge and Mother Aya was the ghost of Dylan's past. Scene after scene, trauma after trauma. My parents telling me they're getting a divorce. My coat being pissed on in the boys' locker room. My mouth being covered while my abuser whispers, "It's okay baby, it's okay." If a Rolodex of pain existed within me, Mother Aya found it and was calling every number.

My sobbing turned into a full-bodied howl. A sound I'd never heard myself nor anyone else make. I cried enough tears to fill a bathtub, and then some. Mother Aya finally brought me to my Dylan the Harlot years, and I could see the hurt in Teen Dylan's eyes. "You talk about me like I'm a monster," Teen Dylan told me. She was right. I was trying to diminish that chapter of my life to the extent where Dylan the Harlot was no longer part of me. Her pained tone turned to something more optimistic. "I am obsessed with the version of you now. I think you're really, really cool. I love your videos. You're my hero," Teen Dylan concluded, letting out a rare half smile.

Dylan the Harlot just needed acknowledgment from current me, she needed her transness to be seen. I held her. We laughed. We cried happy tears. And then she threw up.

When I say she, I mean me, but younger me was definitely the one doing the heavy lifting. I had a moment where what came up and out was a frightening amount, where my human self came knocking like, "Girl, do you need a hospital?" My belly was inverted, and I knew every ounce of pain and every piece of gum was in the bucket in front of me. I collapsed on the cot and Alyssa ran over with water. I couldn't keep it down at first, but it finally settled. When I knew nothing other than words would come out of my mouth, I looked up at Alyssa and said, "I can't do this again tomorrow." There was zero sense of shame in that decision.

"We can talk about it in the morning," Alyssa said. She tried to walk me home, but I, once again, assured her I was okay. When I got back to my room, Dylan the Harlot and I collapsed into bed, together at last.

The next morning, my reflection in the mirror was alarming. My body was giving Bella in *Breaking Dawn Part I.* You know the part where her bones were breaking because her vampire baby was taking all her nutrients? Yeah, no more ayahuasca for me. I called the Marriott and scheduled a last-minute massage, packed a day bag, and went to talk to Alyssa. When she saw my bag, she knew my intentions right away.

"Are you sure you don't want to try for tonight?" she asked.

"I got everything I needed! Be back in a bit!" I said, as I raced out the door with hotel brunch on my mind.

The intention for the final night was supposed to honor my future self, and I decided to do just that with an umbrella drink. I didn't even feel bad. I had no more vomit to give.

This trip gave me a break from the Dark Thoughts, and now, almost a year later, I realize my relationship with them has changed.

What I went for was answers, and what I left with was hope. While the answers weren't as definitive as I'd wanted them to be, they left my spiritual side with enough to work with. It was almost like, "What a shame this would be, to not see life play out like it's supposed to." I felt less alone. I'd glimpsed into my purpose. Even if this Mother Aya figure was a piece of my self-conscious state of being, at least I had something to go off of. During that week the number of times I experienced suicidal ideation was . . . zero. That made this trip worth it right there.

That night, in lieu of another ceremony, Alyssa and I ended up at a cerveceria chugging beers out of tavern mugs. The sweetness to life is so unexpected. Maybe I should try more fruit.

* * * * *

Packing up my suitcase, which was now slightly heavier from the jackets and blankets I purchased out of sheer freezing-ness, I knew I wasn't ready to give up my city-girl sparkle for a life off the grid. Maybe one day I'll pull an Alyssa and move down here, but I was excited to return home to see what the future held in the aftershocks of the plant medicine.

DAY 156 of being a girl . . .

. . . And I went to church. I miss God. Ever since I left Catholic school, my relationship to a higher power has been half-baked and messy. Was my belief in God ever pure and all mine? I was handed down these ideals and stories by my family, starting at my baptism, so the majority of church visits were made against my will. I had only attended church by choice a few times in college with frequent churchgoers Bryn and Frankie because I had the Sunday Scaries and FOMO. I did join the LIGHT group, which was a student-led group for musical theater majors who believed in God to gather once a week and talk about a Bible verse. I was happily surprised to see a few of the other gay boys in there, impressed we were able to hang on to an ounce of faith with our sinful sexual orientation. After college I lost my connection to the church, and ever since I transitioned, I have felt even less drawn to attend a house of worship.

Don't get me wrong; I've felt a higher power's presence over the past few years. I especially see God in nature. I see transness in nature too. Colors of flowers that seem so vibrant they must be unnatural, untouched mountains that look carved by master sculptors, a bird's call that doesn't match their appearance. One of my dreams in life is to rent out a huge mega cabin in the woods and fill it with trans folks to have a summer camp redo, where we make lanyards and paddle canoes. I bet I would feel God somewhere like that.

Lately, I've been feeling a little nostalgic for the structure and dullness of Catholic mass. I sort of miss the archaic Bible verses that would be read in monotone by a man in an unflattering dress, and how I'd have to interpret the words to fit whatever was going on in my life that week. There were a few times when the readings would be suspiciously specific (say *that* ten times fast) to what I was trying to navigate. I also missed having the Communion wafer and wine, because I always treated it like snack time. Today, I had the urge to find God in a formal setting.

My dad still attends Catholic mass every Sunday in San Diego; I could definitely go with him, but I don't love the idea of unearthing the childhood trauma Catholicism caused me. My mom goes to a new-age Christian church with a rock band, but I'd bet you a hundred bucks a few of its attendees are not fans of my content. Hard pass on hers too. Feels like a fresh start kind of moment. I googled "Queer accepting church Los Angeles" to see where my safest option was ("Trans accepting church Los Angeles" felt like too unrealistic). A Unitarian church popped up as the first result, and the website's homepage had a rainbow flag on it, which was good enough for me. I put on a dress that I wore to a gay wedding a few months before, grabbed my goose purse, and went on my mother Mary way.

The Unitarian church looked regal from the outside, but on the inside, it felt a little more like a middle school auditorium flexi space. I was definitely one of the younger attendees, but not the quirkiest. There were colorful suspenders, crazy hair dye jobs, and every person was wearing a mask, impressive since most of LA had sort of thrown in the towel on Covid protocol. I was grateful to be a part of them.

What followed was one of the most wackadoodle religious experiences I've ever witnessed. There was no set pastor; rather, the church members shared in leading the worship, and there was no shortage of speakers who got up on that stage. Their sermons were passionate and from the heart, though a few felt like monologues from soap operas. I wouldn't be surprised if one or two of them were actors running their lines. Hey, a stage is a stage.

Instead of Holy Communion, they had a bowl that you would place a rock in with a silent joy or sorrow you wanted to share. I decided to not stand up, as I wanted to keep a low profile while I sussed the place out. My silent joy was owning my adulthood and meeting God somewhere new. As the service concluded, I did feel that yummy pride when you do something that you know the world values as "good." Went to church, check!

I don't think the Unitarian church is going to be a regular haunt for me, but I do think it was a good stepping stone. I called my mom when I got home, and she was thrilled to hear that I went somewhere Jesus-y.

I get this inkling that Dana is scared I am going to become a Hollywood satanic worshipper, so the more I can remind her of my faith, the less anxious she is.

I'm beginning to think that there are a lot of different ways to have a relationship with God. Maybe God could have a bigger connection with my transition than I would've suspected. With that, I thought I would share a little bedtime prayer with you:

Dear God,

Thank you for reconnecting with me. I have a feeling I need you more now than ever, especially as I'm finding myself in some pretty intense situations. I'm almost positive that you don't hate trans people. Every day, this feels less like a curse and more like a blessing. I hope you approve of the woman I am becoming, that I keep going viral, and also that I don't post anything that would make you upset. Hell, I even made a video about you today, which I feel should win me some brownie points up there. Please send me someone really nice to kiss on a regular basis. No huge rush, but soon would be awesome. Keep doin' your thing.

LOVE YA,

Dylan

DAY 172 of being a girl . . .

. . . And I'm going to pick out my new face. Kidding, but what I wanted from FFS was essentially that. FFS stands for facial feminization surgery, and it is a form of gender-affirming care for trans-feminine people to soften our facial features. The procedure is done by skilled plastic surgeons, and I knew I wanted the best of the best. From my comprehensive research (multiple nights of scrolling trans Reddit threads), I've gathered that Dr. Harrison Lee was the most coveted FFS specialist by fellow dolls. I followed him on Instagram, and the next day I got a DM from his nurse saying Dr. Lee would be happy to have me come in for a consultation if I was interested. This is where I've felt my privilege most: getting access to gender-affirming care has been relatively swift and available to me because of my platform. Also on Reddit, I read notes from trans gals who wait years to get their consults, some who have to pursue sex work in order to cover high costs, and others who have given up hope of getting procedures done because of their lack of insurance. It's such a fucked-up system, and depending on how you look at it, I either am part of the problem or I outsmarted it altogether. I sat with those two binaries and decided

that most would capitalize on this consultation offer, so I responded to their DM. "Yes, please."

I've had three weeks to stare into the mirror in preparation for the consultation. I knew that I wasn't happy with my reflection, but now the opportunity for tangible change was upon me. When I look in the mirror before bed, especially in full glam, I see the woman that I am, but as the face wash melts off the layers of time and effort I put in to feminize, I see remnants of manhood that stare back: the large chin and jaw that resembled Jim Carrey in *The Mask* much more than

Audrey Hepburn in *Breakfast at Tiffany's*, the forehead and brow bone that walk into a room before I do, the Adam's apple that moves up and down every time I go to share my story, and we all know by now that I hate fruit.

I do wonder if my image wasn't so public if I'd still feel as called to make these changes (and fast). But a very visible existence seems to be my new normal. If I'm going to give the public so much of myself to be heavily scrutinized, I might as well give myself what I need in return. **Cue: "Something to Talk About."**

Today's the day! How does one glam for a plastic surgeon consult? I didn't want to shape-shift so hard that Dr. Lee minimized what procedures I needed, but I also didn't want to go in barefaced, because we were filming together. I settled for foundation, a light coat of mascara, and a pink lipstick, not overlining my lips.

When I arrived at Dr. Lee's office in Beverly Hills, I sat in the waiting room alongside another woman, her face covered in bandages.

A Conversation in Dr. Lee's Waiting Room

Waiting Woman Through Swollen Lips: Girl, I recognize you from the internet.

Me: Oh, hi!

WWTSL: Doll to doll, you're seeing the best. Dr. Lee is going to turn you out. I just had revisions from my first FFS with a different doctor. I shoulda just went to Lee first. What are you having done?

Me: I'm not entirely sure yet! This is my first consult, so I'm just going to see what he thinks.

WWTSL: Do it all in one go, if you can afford it. This recovery is rough. I'm a week out.

I was so thankful for this woman. It felt like I had a new friend, one who was in the trenches before me. We continued chatting until a nurse called my name. I said bye before getting her name but wished her a happy healing journey.

"Hiiii, honey!" The nurse, gorgeously made up with lashes and glowing skin, hugged me once we were in the exam room. This was Vilma, my new queen. I love a hug with a stranger. "I've been watching your whole journey since Day 1 and was SO excited when you followed us. You are so beautiful and funny and sweet. We are going to just enhance all of that. Dr. Lee will be right in," she told me as she snapped some "before" shots on a background and then floated out of the room.

I sat thinking about the woman in the waiting room and realized that would be me. Was I ready to see myself swollen in bandages? Was the world ready to see me swollen in bandages?

Before my spiral could take me any deeper, Dr. Lee came through the door. The man, the myth, the legend. He had done FFS for numerous famed trans women over the years, including a member of the Kardashian clan, whom I had recently had a public internet spat with. I was initially worried that he might hold that against me, as I didn't know if FFS doctors took sides, but I decided he probably was profesh enough to play Switzerland.

A Conversation with Dr. Lee

Dr. Lee: You've already got beautiful structure, great cheekbones, nothing too pronounced.

Damn! Maybe I was about to walk out of here with no surgery necessary!

Me: So would you do anything?

Dr. Lee: Well . . . I would shave the brow bone off, lift the eyebrows, take down the hairline a few inches, do a rhinoplasty to bring down the width of the nose, lift the lip, possibly small cheek implants, I would take the chin in and shave the jaw, and shave the trachea off.

Okay, so he would do something.

Out of all the laundry list, there were two things that worried me most: the nose job and the trachea shave.

Me: If I get a nose job, won't it look like I've had work done?

Dr. Lee: I mean . . . yes. You will look different.

Me: Could I not get a nose job but all the other things?

Dr. Lee: You can, but it might be less of a full transformation.

Me: And the tracheal shave—I'm a singer. That sounds terrifying.

Dr. Lee: I can go conservative on your tracheal shave.

I thought about the Broadway musicals I had been auditioning for and the upcoming Day 365 show I was plotting for March. My voice was my most precious cargo.

"Okay. SUPER conservatively. And the cheek implants—do I need those?"

"It's up to you."

"Get the cheek implants, honey, you'll love 'em," Vilma chimed in behind her clipboard, where she'd been writing down everything the doctor was rattling off.

"Okay. When would I be able to come in for surgery?" I asked, nervous for the answer, knowing it could be years.

"When do you want to?" Dr. Lee asked.

"Um . . . is December too soon?" I sheepishly ask.

"I was thinking next month, but we can wait until December, no problem. Vilma will get you a date."

We filmed a video together for my *Days of Girlhood*, and Dr. Lee left to attend to the next doll.

Vilma pulled up the schedule and asked if December 16 worked.

"YES! Perfect!" That was the Friday the entertainment industry shuts down for the holidays, and I could heal over Christmas and my birthday, ready to hit it in the New Year. I paid a down payment then and there and walked out, passing by another bandaged patient in the waiting room. "You're gonna look AMAZING!" I whispered as I walked past. There was something magical in Dr. Lee's office air, probably gender euphoria and pain meds. In just three months I'd be the one in the bandages, hyping up the next nervous girl there for her consult. I can't wait.

LOVE YA,

Dylan ♡

DAY 221 of being a girl . . .

. . . And today I am going to the White House to talk
to the president of the United States. This would be a
big win for most, but I'm currently navigating a social
media shitstorm over a beauty podcast where I talked
about womanhood. The discourse has me off my game.
For all the crying I did last night, I don't look so bad.
Crying seems to be a common theme these days. Don't
read the comments, dammit! I wonder how the haters will
feel about today's interview. I'm guessing they won't
be thrilled. *But promise me something? No matter what
happens, will you please try to enjoy this? I hate how
your wins lately turn sour.* You deserve an Elle Woods
moment today. But I beg of you, don't fuck this up, Dyl.
This is the kind of place I'd like to be invited back.

To be honest, politics scare the SHIT out of me. In
some ways, I feel like I was forced into activism by
simply being trans. Every trans person has to master
the art of overexplaining themselves and be on the
ready to defend their existence at the drop of a hat.

My distaste for politics stems from a fear of
confrontation. I am the first to distance myself from
any sort of fight, and also the first to apologize (even if it
wasn't my fault) just to smooth anything and everything
over. I'm wildly liberal, but my aversion to confrontation

also keeps me curious to know if there's any chance of understanding each other, any glimmer of hope.

When it comes to transness, I have my go-to talking points, but I am nowhere near as versed as the many incredible activists in our community. So, it came as a SHOCK when I got this call from my agent.

A Conversation with My Agent

Agent: A news station would like to send you to the White House to interview the president next week, specifically about trans rights.

Me: Wrong number!

Agent: Hear me out. It's going to be an open conversation. Don't worry, you won't be alone. There are five other speakers to cover different topics.

Me: What are the other topics?

Agent: Gun control, abortion access, climate change, incarceration, and debt crisis.

Me: Oh. Wow.

Agent: It could be a really cool opportunity. I don't think a lot of influencers get asked to do something like this. Can I tell them you're in?

My mind was racing. They must have made a mistake. I do think I'm making an impact in the world on some level, but this is not some sixty-second TikTok video where I can chat to the camera in my canopy bed. I'd be chatting to one of the most powerful men in the world, and not shooting the shit—I'd be representing an entire community that I am only just stepping into. Before my concerns could catch up to my mouth, I simply said, "Surrreeee."

And the whirlwind began, starting with an initial call with the producers of the news segment. "Are you POSITIVE you picked the right person?" I asked them.

"Definitely!"

"Okay, but . . . why me?"

"First, you'll draw in a young audience. But most importantly, you are already accustomed to the hate from the far right; we don't want to subject a trans person who's not used to that, since it can get pretty brutal. And, last, you're optimistic. Biden is a very hopeful guy, and all these topics are heavy. You'll add a touch of positivity to the room that I think we all need."

That made me feel a little bit better. If it meant another trans person didn't get meme'd by far-right media, I'd happily be the meme. I might be the silliest version of a presidential reporter, but I vowed to myself that I would do my absolute best to show up for my trans fam. This isn't about a cute visit to DC, it's about calling out these anti-trans legislators and their dookie anti-trans laws.

I still had to be approved by the White House, and I think they did a pretty hefty background check before they agreed to let me come. I was a little surprised they cleared me. After trespassing in a graveyard, forging my parents' signatures many a time, and adopting a wild opossum, I thought the government would raise some eyebrows. I'd love to know if they found any good dirt, because I bet the White House background check is, like, as comprehensive as it gets.

For a few weeks leading up to my journalistic debut, I had a series of follow-up meetings with the producers to help me shape my questions for the president. We had to be wickedly specific and cautious in wording, so that transphobes couldn't use any of my own words against me. My videos had already fallen victim to extremist scrutiny plenty of times, like my "normalize the bulge" jingle (FML), so I was gonna be on high alert to not give them anything good. I also called my TikTok friend Erin Reed, who covers trans legislation on her page, and Jonathan Van Ness, who is very active in the community, to help form my questions.

Just as I was picking out which outfit to wear for the interview, I get another call. "Dylan, do you want to audition for Glinda on Broadway?" YES, I DO. "Great, the audition is on October 18!" That is the same day as my interview with the president. I was absolutely in the greatest Dyl pickle of my life.

Playing Glinda is my biggest dream ever, but I knew that I probably couldn't call up Joe Biden and ask him to reschedule so that I could go sing and dance. *Wicked* has been running for almost twenty years, so as much as it kills me, it probably isn't leaving anytime soon. The White House it is.

I was flown coach to DC, so at least we know tax dollars aren't going to my comfort. I spent all morning in hair and makeup, and my hair stylist was a trans woman who put my mind at ease. "Oh, he's gonna love you. Politicians love trans girls. They love us around here." I raised an eyebrow. She told me about the different parts of town and the DC bars that the closeted conservative politicians liked to frequent. We laughed, and then I practiced my questions for Joe over and over again.

I hired a stylist, and we came up with a pretty fierce outfit with the trans flag colors. I went with pants, which felt kinda like a serve. I did make sure to tuck my bits away extra well so that Twitter couldn't spout off about my crotch. These are the things I often worry about. I wore a pink blouse that was an extension of my femininity. It was giving Stanford Blatch at his wedding vibes. Blue flared pants, a nod to my love of retro fashion. A white vintage cape jacket tied the look together with a crystal belt. Maybe the cape will make me feel like a hero and a little less like a mediocre, ill-equipped reporter.

In the lobby of the hotel, I met the other five interviewers, each of whom had a specific tie to the legislation topic they were tackling. Traumatic experiences like school shootings and wrongful incarceration had led them to this moment, which had me questioning my worthiness of invite once again. All of them were so kind, and we ran over our questions and practiced being the president for one another. Before the White House, we had to visit an offsite office to get Covid tested. I had taken quite a few tests before, but this one I was especially terrified to fail.

All clear!

We arrived at the White House, and the building itself did feel as majestic as one might imagine. More like a museum than a house. I was planning to film anything and everything but was greeted with an unpleasant discovery. "No filming outside or inside," said the first Secret Service person I came in contact with. I did end up taking a few little clips, but I didn't want to be that bitch who got thrown out of the White House for making a TikTok, ya feel me?

I wasn't allowed to use the restroom or drink water without a Secret Service escort following me. What I would've given to snoop through some drawers.

The interview took place in the East Room, which is extra special because it's attached to President Biden's private living quarters. Six of us in a semicircle of chairs, facing one empty chair where the big man would sit. We waited for over an hour, in silence—you could hear a pin drop. Apparently, he had some official business that pushed our time slot back. The only sound was whispers from staff saying, "He's exiting the Oval Office . . . he's thirty seconds out . . . entering now."

And there he was. Mr. Joe Biden, standing right in front of me. He shook each of our hands and stopped when he got to me.

A Conversation with President Biden

President Biden: I was chatting with my friend about you today.

He said this with a relaxed notion, as if he were Lily nonchalantly gabbing with her mom about me.

Me: Oh really? What's their name?

I had never asked a question faster, and I had never needed an answer more in my life.

President Biden: I'll tell you in a minute.

And he continued to greet the rest of the room, as I stood stunned that he even knew who I was. Who was this mystery friend he was talking about? Oprah? The Pope? Talk about conversational blue balls. I feared I might never find out.

As we got started, the room was a bit tense, but I was distracted by his gorgeous baby blue eyes. Am I allowed to say that? We were moments away from filming when he looked directly at me and said, "Sarah McBride?"

"What?"

"Sarah McBride is the friend I was talking about earlier. We chatted on the phone about you today."

Sarah is a trans senator in Delaware and the first openly transgender person to work in the White House, while she was an intern. I'd actually just followed Sarah on Instagram that morning, because my hair stylist told me about her. (And I can confirm they did speak about me; Sarah sent me a DM shortly after the interview telling me so!!) Before Joe and I could talk more, it was showtime.

I was the third speaker of six, which is a great spot in both politics and stand-up comedy. The crowd is warmed up but isn't fatigued yet. As the first two speakers went, I tried to listen to their questions, but I kept forgetting my own and looking down to my note cards. In stand-up, sometimes the best jokes come completely unplanned, but I didn't think this was the gig for riffing.

I fully blacked out while the president and I were talking, but I remember being so moved by his support of the trans community that I had to stop myself from getting emotional. I wasn't here to cry, I was here to be a hard-hitting reporter, dammit! While he didn't answer my questions too specifically, he said he had our back. I just hope he will keep his promises.

He spoke with strength but also kindness, power but also empathy. This was the first time in my life that I wasn't afraid of politics. It was like finding the courage to look under the bed for monsters and seeing

that there weren't any there. I'm sure there were a few skeletons locked in the linen closet, but dare I say I was proud to be an American lol. For one brief second, I actually had a spark go off in my head that I might want to explore becoming a politician one day.

Up until this point, I pictured myself the first lady. But now, I think about how fierce it would be to have a trans woman for president. Not me, obvi, but like . . . maybe a Sarah McBride?! We're probably gonna need a few cis women in there first, but maybe one day. It did feel a little eerie being there, seeing all the photos of old white men on the wall, and thinking how sad it was that this country hasn't experienced a woman at its helm. But if it has to be an old white man, I guess I'm cool with it being Joe.

Once the full interview concluded, we took some pictures, and he asked us if we'd like to see the Oval Office. I screamed "YES!" Joe's staff was visibly like "what the fuck" when he offered this; I'm assuming he had other appointments. He is the president after all.

Joe led us through different rooms, pointing at every photo and painting and telling us about the subject. I was the most animated of the six of us, so I did most of the talking. He put his arm around me, and I told him about the drama that was currently happening because of the beauty podcast I was on. He said, "Don't listen to any of that." Okay, Joe. I know we aren't supposed to seek validation from men, but having the validation of the president? I was walking on air.

My favorite room that he showed us was the movie theater.

As soon as we walked in, my eyes got big and my voice got loud with excitement. "This place is giant! You could do a musical in here!"

"I can't, but you definitely could." He laughed.

I knew what must be done. I broke out into a short eight count of dance right there on the spot. I had been recycling specific choreography from the Cathedral Catholic dance team audition ten years prior. I didn't make the team, but that choreo had made its way to MANY a dance floor. This time, in the White House movie theater. For the president of the United States of America. Lily makes fun of me because she's seen it a thousand different times, with little crowds of people cheering on my impressive moves. Who's laughing now, Lil? Joe loved it!

Once we were in the Oval Office, which to my surprise is NOT a cardboard set on a soundstage but, in fact, an actual office, I asked the president if he had a dog. Joe called his Secret Service agent to go get his German shepherd Commander. They brought Commander in, and I lay on the carpet petting him while he licked my face. I so wish I had had my phone for at least that moment to capture. I looked over to the official photographer, whom I begged to snap a photo. She begrudgingly took a single shot. If anyone from the White House is reading this, I would LOVE this pic please and thank you.

At this point I'd been with Joe for nearly three hours, and his staff was alerting him of a meeting with a leader of another country that he was late to. When we said our goodbyes, he gave me a cookie that was wrapped with a gold seal. He and I don't see eye to eye on everything, and this visit (or the cookie) does not pardon him from my critiques past or present, but I respected him that day.

When I arrived back at my hotel room, I lay down, exhausted, staring up at the ceiling. I don't think that was my gig. A wave of guilt rushes over me— hoping the trans community won't be disappointed. I think next time I make a DC visit I would rather lead with one of my strengths—like singing at a Kennedy Center Honors event or something a little bit more my speed. These moments are important for me to take stock of, so I don't continuously say yes to things that aren't for me. But, a trans woman interviewing the president is . . . major. And I'm sure it will invoke some majorly negative press. But how about, just for tonight, as I fall asleep, I'll try and let it be a win.

LOVE YA,

Dylan

Chapter 6

CELEBRITY 2.0

2001. A dark stage. San Diego, CA.

Cue: "The Boy from New York City"

Ooh wah, ooh wah cool, cool kitty.

LIGHTS UP, A LINE OF FORTY GIRLS, AGES 4–5, CLING TO EACH OTHERS' WAISTS AS THEY SHUFFLE ONTO STAGE IN TINY PATENT LEATHER TAP SHOES AND SEQUIN TUTUS.

Tell us about the boy from New York City.

AT THE BACK OF THE LINE, ONE GIRL (WHO LOOKS A LOT LIKE A BOY) FOLLOWS THE REST, WEARING A SEQUIN VEST AND PANTS

Ooh wah, ooh wah cool, cool kitty.

THE GIRLS CIRCLE AROUND THE VESTED CHILD WHILE VESTED CHILD SHUFFLES IN PLACE CENTER STAGE.

Tell us about the boy from New York City.

THE CROWD GOES WILD.

I feel seen. Being onstage as the only boy in Diane's School of Dance recitals was a surefire way to get looks in my direction, but I so desperately wanted to be one of the girls in the sequin tutus. No one told me I was supposed to love the spotlight, and any expectations were put there by myself. Sure, my parents told me to get straight As, but I was the one forcing myself to fill my days with extracurriculars, part-time jobs, and auditions. The expectations on myself were nowhere near as high as they are now, because I didn't think I'd amount to anything close to famous. I was in the wrong body. I was abusing it in different ways to numb my gender dysphoria. But as I slowly discovered transness, my creativity grew in tandem. I was getting ideas like little divine revelations. "Make this video," "Sing this song," "Pitch this concept," and when I came out as nonbinary, I was off to the races.

I had two internet series before *Days of Girlhood*. I had *Interviewing Animals with Dylan* and *It's a They! Question of the Day*. Neither really took off. But I was putting in the effort. I was creating, but still finding my footing. When *Days of Girlhood* began, the first day of publicly living my truth, the world saw me. And as I continued living in my truth, they kept seeing me. And the ideas kept coming. Because each divine idea I answered and executed felt like a miracle. Like every time I went to make something, little Dylan got to take off the vest and put on the tutu, and there was no longer the one, lone Boy from New York City, but rather a forty-first little tap-dancing gal.

I pictured my creative process on social media as an assembly line, where I build my invention, package it, and send it out to consumers every single day. When Beergate happened, the assembly line screeched to a halt. The conveyor belt got backed up, and the only way I could fix it was by speaking my truth. When I did finally share my story, the assembly line didn't quite go back to the same rapid speed as before. New fears and anxieties were caught in the gears and the only things I could manufacture were frivolous lip-sync audios or photos of me looking glam. Where did the wise, funny, vulnerable moments go?

Being a good person has never been harder than it is right now. The internet is rewarding bad behavior at an all-time high. Narcissists have caught on to therapy talk to masquerade selfishness as self-care. We are platforming problematic people merely because they are adding to the pop culture zeitgeist and lining their pockets while they get the last laugh. Why shouldn't we all just lean into chaos if kindness is becoming untrendy? To that I say: TGFM.

Thank God for Mory. I can't stress just how much she has saved my life. When I felt the pressures of fame beginning to weigh on me in 2022 and I was struggling mentally, I reached out to contacts in the industry to see if anyone knew of a therapist who worked with folks in the spotlight. No one had an immediate "this is who you need" other than a few psychic recommendations, which I normally would welcome with open arms, but this depression felt like it needed a stronger cure than just a rough estimate of when I'd find love.

So, when in doubt: Ask the queers. They have the best taste in everything else, and why wouldn't that include mental health professionals?! I found myself on a one-on-one friend date for the first time with Alok Vaid-Menon, an iconic speaker, writer, actor, and comedian. Their internet presence was a bit intimidating to me because they had offered me so many prophetic moments through Instagram reels, and I didn't want to say anything dumb in front of them. I opened up to Alok before the appetizers were even served, and by the time the entrees were finished I knew I had found one of those people who would change my perspective on the world forever. Cherish those ones, it's not often they come around. On that first-friend-date, I felt safe enough to ask Alok about a therapist, and without responding, they pulled out their phone and started typing. I waited. "What's your email?" they asked without looking up. "You need Mory."

Within a week of that dinner, I was Zooming with Mory, life coach to the stars. Mory is a dark-haired beauty who looks like she stepped out of an oil painting from Jesus's time. Her smile made me feel safe, and her maternal energy jumped off the screen. Mory isn't a licensed therapist, which is great because we're allowed to drink together and go on vacations! Mory and I started working together seven months before Beergate, so when that tsunami hit, she was my first call. But prior to that drama, I came to her because being seen on a huge scale didn't feel so great, and I was scared that if I didn't do some serious adjusting, I'd end up becoming:

A) A horrible person
B) An addict
C) A person who means well but has no boundaries

Within that first session, I was crying over my career to Mory on Zoom. It became obvious to us both that I needed a new playbook, one where I could write my own rules to being a woman who is SEEN. Mory calls this playbook "Celebrity 2.0."

Celebrity 1.0 is based on the idea that celebrities are often projecting a persona that is meticulously constructed (usually by managers, agents, and PR professionals) and not aligned to their truths. This was how I was operating before Mory; trying to uphold the version of myself that people were responding to positively. Straying from that meticulously constructed persona was terrifying because you couldn't predict the response it would have. I'll never forget the first time I cursed in a TikTok—you'd think, based on the comments section, that I had killed someone's dog. I put myself in a box and served it to millions of people each and every day in pink wrapping, with not a piece of tape showing or a corner out of place. I would've put seasonal department store wrapping associates to shame. But the truth is, I really belong in a box with hot ladies on the wrapping paper and banged-up corners and tape sticking out the side that arrives two weeks after scheduled delivery.

Celebrity 1.0 is alive and thriving everywhere. Earlier this year, a beloved celeb entered my life. I grew up a big fan of hers, so when she invited me over for a one-on-one dinner, I was extremely ecstatic. What I quickly realized was that the only reason I was there was so that she could get a feature on my TikTok page. She misgendered me throughout the evening, which she would beat herself up about, but then do it again and again. It was sad to see someone I admired so deeply fall off the pedestal I had put them on. What I realized while spending time with her was that the more desperate we are to be seen, the harder it becomes to see what is right in front of us. I was standing right there, I knew she didn't see me, and there was nothing I could do to pull her out of her Celebrity 1.0 box. I did not put her on my TikTok. Yay boundaries!

Celebrity 2.0 is the idea that when famous folks are present, real, and committed to their truth, navigating fame will eventually feel less isolating; this leaves room for a longer, happier life and career. There was a brief moment, at the start of *Days of Girlhood*, when I was personifying Celebrity 2.0 without even being aware of its sentiments. In those early days, I couldn't have been shouting my truths any louder. And I would've kept navigating life in the spotlight this way if it weren't for the flood of criticism and comparison. I quickly gave in to the comforts of Celebrity 1.0.

Nothing about my success was constructed at the start, and still, so often, it's just me in my bedroom plotting how to get to the next dream. Conservatives like to think trans people are being created in advertising boardrooms to corrupt stereotypical family living, but that couldn't be further from the truth. At the time of writing this, there are still so few famous trans folks, and those of us who have "made it" really do feel like one in a million. My experience was far more privileged than most, but I gotta give credit to my work ethic. Being famous was never part of the plan, so if I'm going to live it, I might as well find the least toxic version of fame possible. **Cue: Frank Sinatra's "My Way."**

Most of my calls with Mory start with a spiral over that day's rock and a hard place.

"A trans elder I look up to said I didn't phrase this right in my video."

"I didn't look closely enough at my merch roll-out, and the sizing isn't inclusive."

"The bomb threats, Mory, the bomb threats!"

She always calmly responds, "Remember what we talked about?"

Me (metaphorically blacking out, no time for her riddles): "No, Mory, I don't remember!"

"Celebrity 2.0," she follows, with her nagging mama bear energy.

Sometimes I think I am the worst possible person to be chosen for this lifestyle. I feel things WAY too hard—and when life moves this fast, I can find myself in multiple fires a day. My body doesn't know when to snap out of adrenaline mode. I want to fix everything instantly.

Finding others in the spotlight has helped me immensely. Friendships with sparkly celebrity women has given me data to help me trek forward.

I was with a sparkly new friend at Sundance Film Festival. They hadn't seen any of my content, which felt like a breath of fresh air. They asked me to give them the SparkNotes version, which went something like:

"I made a comedic coming-out video as a woman, transitioned a little too close to the sun, took a beer campaign that burned me, and now I'm generally sad . . . ish."

To which they replied:

"You were slain."

"What?"

"You were slain and now you are recovering from the slay."

It made me giggle because gen z'ers and the queer community have kidnapped the term *slay* as the highest form of compliment, but this gen x'er meant it at its most definitive form. "All humans go through horrible things, deaths, breakups, etc. . . . but there's only a few of us who have been truly slain. The percentage becomes higher the more notable you become."

They told me about their personal slay moment, which took them down in the media many years prior. I had heard about it but was too young to remember it when it was happening. "Well, when did you feel fully healed from it?" I asked.

"This week. Picking up my credentials at Sundance. I felt full."

This killed the part of me that wanted to fix things FAST. Looks like slay-healing is going to take a lot longer than the one to two weeks I had scheduled. They asked me about the things I would like to do going forward, which was a nice break from harping on the past for people who just wanted to hear about my trauma. I perked up and shared my ideas for the future. "That. There. Find the creativity," this new friend kindly instructed. "Hold on to it and don't let it go. That will help heal you."

Another Celebrity 2.0 sighting was when a different sparkly friend invited me to their bougie London apartment for lunch, during a time when they too were going through a slay. We both shared our slays over pasta and held hands. After two hours of conversation, they stood up.

"I hope you don't mind; I just need a little something," and she pulled out a box of joints.

I was supposed to have my first dialect coaching over Zoom for a big callback, but getting stoned with this shiny gal was once in a lifetime. While we lit up, I told her about the coach I was working with, and she goes, "Oh, I love her, I used her for one of my films! Let's call her." Seconds later, she was on the phone with my dialect coach. "Dylan is going to be late to your coaching. We're smoking! Sorry! We love you!" And so we smoked.

Watching this woman let go, her stress melting away, was like watching Celebrity 1.0 convert to 2.0 in real time. Not saying weed is a good fix, maybe even the opposite, but it seemed to really work for her. The conversation changed. Our voices dropped. She started to get real. "Do you think kids should really be allowed to take hormones?" she asked me, as a friend, not an activist.

Normally, this would trigger my alarms, but I felt like we were on a level playing field. There was mutual respect. So, I engaged. "Yeah, I do. What do you want to know?" We talked about my bottom surgery plans. We laughed about my horrible dating stories. We talked about suicidal thoughts. She grabbed me by the shoulders, looked me directly in the eyes, and said, "Don't you dare let them take all of this magic away. You fucking fight. And I will fight. But you have got to remind yourself every day that you were put here on this earth to change people's minds, and it's going to be hard but it's going to be beautiful. Okay?" The way she asked me "okay" was as if my life depended on me hearing her. I heard her. I showed up late and high to my dialect coaching, but I was filled with pasta and fight. Nothing in my life has hit quite as good as my favorite Hollywood idols giving me a pep talk complete with tears and hugs. Cameo could never.

* * * * *

Whenever I meet with a new sparkly woman, I run back to Mory, and she listens to me retell the escapades with that "I told you so" look in her eye, as if she already knew which ladies were stuck in 1.0 and which were in their 2.0 realness. She always asks me, "What'd you learn?" So we can turn the gossip into constructive lessons.

"I've learned to find my truths and continuously remind myself of them when I start to stray."

Then she asks me to run through those truths.

So here are my crystalized truths, the ones that existed before my following, and the ones that will help me continue on my Celebrity 2.0 journey:

I believe miracles are possible.

I believe we are all equal.

I am the student, not the teacher.

I want to find a connection to everything and everyone.

I won't fight fire with fire. I will fight it with love.

I would like to wear the sparkly tutu over the vest, please.

There are forty-one girls from New York City in tap shoes.

DAY 226 of being a girl . . .

. . . And mama mia (here we go again!).

I am home from Washington, DC, and tonight my Biden interview came out. I skipped throwing any sort of organized viewing party and opted for pajamas and pizza with my friend Ryan. Watching it back, I picked apart all the moments I stumbled with my words or had to reference back to my note cards. I hate watching anything of myself, but I especially cringed at my voice and mannerisms in this. Oh well. I drove home, and my mom called right before bed.

A Conversation with My Mom

Mom: Hi there.

Me: Hi, did you watch the interview?

Mom: I'm in a hotel bathroom, Larry is sleeping in the other room.

Me: Okay, but did you watch it?

Mom: Yes, I saw pieces of it. Pretty crazy.

Me: What did you think?

Mom: I thought you came across very professionally. I liked the pantsuit outfit.

Me: Thanks. Any other thoughts?

Mom: Well . . . we're all proud of you, and we do support you, but . . . we can't support you speaking out about children.

Me: What are you talking about?

Mom: In the Biden interview . . . you talked about kids becoming trans . . . it's just not right.

My stomach sank, realizing the gravity of the situation. Here's my mom, a parent of a very influential trans person, who doesn't believe kids should transition. Maybe there's some hope here, let's circle back.

Me: You don't think kids should be allowed to transition?

Mom: I don't. They should have to wait until they're eighteen. Parents and doctors are pushing surgeries and pills on these poor kids, and most of them change their minds. Think of your nieces and nephew. It's heartbreaking.

Me: Where are you getting this information from? That kids are getting surgery? Or that most change their minds? That's the biggest fucking lie I've ever heard.

She knows I mean business when I curse. She HATES when I curse.

Mom: This is where I stand. It's how the family feels.

She loves to make group statements.

Me: You do realize that I'm actively trying to protect the rights of all trans people, right? Like this is a part of my purpose? Oh . . . you don't give a shit about trans people. Only me. That's not good enough.

The tears started welling up in my eyes. And then the fear started up. I pictured her appearing on the news sharing her perspective on trans rights.

The level of power that she held hadn't even occurred to me before this convo.

I needed her to know how important this was to me.

I needed her to know this wasn't a "call me tomorrow to make up" kind of argument.

I needed her to know that this situation was bigger than just the two of us.

"If this is how you feel, I can't have you in my life right now," I said, trying to hide the shake in my voice.

"Oh come on, we were just starting to get to a good place."

"And you know how bad my anxiety is and how much bullshit I've been working through. I don't have the capacity to handle this on top of it all."

"I'll call you tomorrow, get some sleep and—"

"No. Please don't call me. I won't answer. I love you, but I need you to know how much this means to me. I need a break from you."

I was feeling pissy and knew that this next thing would really cement in the gravity.

"As of right now, you aren't my mom anymore."

Oh Jesus Christ Dylan, did you really have to go there? With the line you used almost ten years ago in the therapist's office with her? We're realllllly throwing around that "you're not my mom" line pretty willy-nilly.

I could hear her muffled sobs through the phone. I imagined her in a casino resort hotel bathroom, trying not to wake up her husband. I imagined her getting into bed with mascara raccoon eyes because she's not great about washing off her makeup. Like mother, like daughter. I knew she was feeling BB gun pellets, hitting just below the belt, because I was the one shooting. I may not be a violent person, but I sure knew how to hit hard.

"I will always be your mother. And I love you no matter what."

"I love you too. Please do not contact me. I will reach out to you if and when I'm ready. Good night."

"Night," she choked out.

I feel like such a bitch. Poor gal was living her best life on a vacation and I ruined it. I guess we both ruined things for each other. My White House visit was supposed to be an epic accomplishment, and she managed to make me hate it. What I didn't realize was that the shots fired at her ricocheted right back and hit me just the same. Her pain was also mine. The one person I wanted more than anything to approve of me. Any shred of wanting to go into politics was LONG gone. I'm in my canopy bed now looking up at God and asking them why they are putting me through this. I'm so tired. I just want to be on Broadway.

WHATEVER,

Dylan

DAY 239 of being a girl . . .

. . . And today I got my privilege checked. Thank God for that. Last night, a fellow doll made a video speaking her thoughts about me and my platform. It wasn't anything I hadn't heard before, mostly relating to how unrealistic my journey is compared to the majority of trans folks, but especially Black trans women. I agreed with everything she was saying.

Over these last few months, I've realized that I make trans people feel some kind of way. Whether that feeling is euphoria, or anger, or levity, or disdain. They did not elect me to be our poster child; cis teens and Midwestern moms did. It felt like society plucked me from the dollhouse and I am ready to come home.

Sis Thee Doll is one of the most talented, iconic women I know. I'd seen her in the national tour of *Oklahoma!* playing Ado Annie and knew she was destined for greatness. When her name appeared under the likes of this video critiquing me, I called her up to get some much-needed perspective.

A Conversation with Sis Thee Doll over Facetime

Sis Thee Doll: Hey, girl.

Me: Hey, sis.

I smiled back. We caught up for a bit, and I asked her about the video.

Sis: Yeah girl, I saw it. I agree with a lot of the points made, but just know I love you. I think a lot of us dolls are just tired and would like to see someone with privilege use it for good. They need to see what I can see in you.

Me: How do I show them?

Sis: What are you doing tomorrow?

Sis Thee Doll invited me to a trans march in LA happening the very next day. I couldn't RSVP fast enough.

Arriving at West Hollywood Park, I found Sis among the large group already gathered for the rally. A very sweet trans man approached me and asked me if I would like to speak to the crowd. I knew that my voice was not necessary. I was here to listen. Within the stories shared of deep pain were also stories of love, and hope, and trans joy, and idyllic futures. I realized that my story was just a picture book on display in our community's vast library, and I had some assigned reading to do.

After the rally, we marched on Santa Monica Boulevard, passing my normal frozen yogurt and car wash haunts, but in a sea of dolls blocking traffic. Qween Jean. Blossom Brown. *Supergirl*'s Nicole Maines. These are some of the trailblazing women I got to meet that day. I stared at them in awe. What I saw was more perseverance than humanly possible. **Cue: "YOU CAN'T GET RID OF US, BITCH!"** It was as if the group of us were using our gravitational pull to bring earth closer to planet doll. Maybe we really aren't of this world. We are magic. When I feel alone, or like I'm an alien, or that no one will ever understand why or how I am the way I am, I will think of this moment in gratitude.

I'd like to make a promise to the dolls, and to myself, that no matter where life takes me or for how long I stray, I will always come back to the dollhouse. That I will do my best, and probably fail them a million times, but at the end, I will do right by them a million and one. The pain the world has attempted to put onto us is there to separate, but maybe if I harness my pain to bring me closer to them, to open up to girls like me, to listen, maybe that pain will actually be what brings us closer together. That is what I was shown today.

LOVE YA,

Dylan♥

DAY 282 of being a girl . . .

. . . And I'm giving swollen Frankenstein. Yesterday was my facial feminization surgery, and according to the doctor it went great, but my reflection says otherwise. There are no distinguishable features! It's all just swelling. Did I make a horrible decision?

To calm my spiraling mind, in my OxyContin haze, I open up TikTok:

> Dylan doesn't deserve ffs because . . .

Scroll.

> It's too soon for Dylan to get . . .

Scroll.

> While I'm happy for Dylan to get gender affirming care I personally don't think . . .

Scroll.

My heart sinks.

Time to jump into damage control.

Follow the creators who made the videos.

Message them, begin conversation.

Hear them out. Apologize.

Hate yourself.

Repeat.

Wait, what am I doing?

Do I need to make an apology video?

Nope, nope, nope. Not this time. First of all, I look
way too fucked up, but really this was supposed
to be the one thing this year that was for me and me
alone. If people chose to begin discourse over my
FFS, then let them, but I don't need to subject
myself to these videos. I just wish they wouldn't
tag me in them.

Last night, right after I arrived at the aftercare facility, I was wheeled into the hotel room-turned-hospital
setup and Lily was waiting for me. Her eyes bulged out of
her head, and she let out a small gasp when she saw me.
"He's gonna need plenty of rest," said the nurse. "She!"
Lily corrected her. This happened a few more times,
being misgendered by the nurses. It was almost comical.
I just went through hours of invasive surgery to be
seem more womanly, and no one even batted an eyelash!
By now I've learned that no matter what I do, people will

just keep pushing the finish line back. I'm not running that race. Lily climbed into bed with me and stroked the tiny bloody ponytail popping out of my head bandages.

"I'm Ariana Grande, bitch. Yuh," I said with little inflection. Making Lily laugh was still top of mind even now. Time to get some sleep and tomorrow I'll catch up on some TV. What's everyone been watching?

LOVE YA,

Dylan

Chapter 7

THE KISSING BANDIT

I was really into parts work in therapy for a long time. A million others can and will explain parts work better than I can, but the way I've interpreted it is that we have different versions of ourselves, and we need to get them all synced up so we can be in complete alignment. One of my parts was Woo-Woo Dylan, whom we've met on occasion in this book. My life would look very different if Woo-Woo Dylan was the only version of myself that I was trying to appease. Unfortunately for Woo-Woo Dylan, her slutty twin sister, Party Dylan, exists. I have to give both Dylans equal attention and care or else they'll start to act out. If Party Dylan is hitting it too hard at events, Woo-Woo Dylan will have a panic attack and schedule an emergency session with an overpriced psychic. If Woo-Woo Dylan is getting too granola, Party Dylan will send her on a reckless "let's hit the strip club and text everyone we've ever kissed" spree.

I knew Woo-Woo Dylan and Party Dylan would need to heal from Beergate differently, so I treated the month of July like two separate birthday parties for my twins. Woo-Woo Dylan got a trip to Peru and ayahuasca with a shaman, but that left Party Dylan longing for the dance floor. She would soon get her fill in the form of a trip to the South of France.

On a text thread out of the blue, I received the following from my gal pal friend Liza: "What are y'all up to next week?" Followed by a link to the most gorgeous house I'd ever ever seen. The other member of the group chat was our friend Sabrina, who immediately replied: "I'm free!" I checked my calendar. Nothing. "Me too!" And just like that, a girls' trip was born.

I had just seven days before I needed to arrive in Antibes, France, where the house was located, and I knew exactly where to stop first: London, to see Lily.

* * * * *

"JUST GET HERE NOW!" Lily screams on the FaceTime call when I tell her that I'm going to Europe. We picked out a hotel to have our weeklong slumber party. Although Lily is married, she still is game for a BFF sleepover. When I'm married, I hope I operate like Lily. Weeklong sleepovers.

I left Peru and stopped by LA to unpack and repack before traveling to Europe. I didn't want to have too much time alone with my thoughts, or to let the epic energy I cultivated in Peru shift back to extreme depression, so I kept my time in LA to a minimum. But I knew one thing needed to happen before I crossed the pond—I needed to be blonde.

I had flirted with my Bombshell Era before; putting Rapunzel's hair color on my 2023 vision board, even wearing a blonde wig to the Tony Awards, but I decided it was time for something more permanent. Hair holds energy, and my healthy long brunette locks constantly reminded me of the images I would see of myself in conservative media, the Audrey Hepburn persona I had leaned into for most of my transition. I was the good girl, Jackie O., but I wanted to be the other woman for once, I wanted to be Marilyn. (Plus, all the stress had caused a few premature gray hairs that were going to have to be dyed anyway . . . so no time like the present!)

I knew upkeep was going to be a bitch, and there was no one I trusted with my hair more than Angie, my hair stylist. We scheduled the bleach and tone for July 13, or the national holiday now known as "the day Dylan got SIGNIFICANTLY cuntier." We also dyed my eyebrows. I was not fucking around here. Full commit. I found the sexiest mesh Jean Paul Gaultier dress to premiere my new look, and the rest is history.

Eight hours later, looking in the mirror, I saw Marilyn and not Audrey. I also saw my nipples (the dress was see-through). A sunny little smile shot across my face, but I sucked in my cheeks and pursed my lips to leave behind any remnants of sweetness. I was no longer the trans beer girl. I didn't know who I was, but at least I wasn't her.

As I headed to the airport, I was struck with an intense realization: I needed sex desperately. It had been four years, and I was beginning to think that I might have been cursed by a homophobic sex witch. I was a twink before Troye Sivan types were seen as thee moment, so pre-transition I didn't pull incredibly hard in bed. And I looked a little rough in my nonbinary/early transition era, but now that I was a blonde and my tits didn't need a magnifying glass to be seen, it felt like a good time to jump back in the dating pool. I set my Raya profile to London and updated my photos to reflect my new 'do.

Arriving to the hotel and seeing Lily, my favorite blonde, waiting for me in the lobby was like déjà vu. It seems like every time I find myself in uncharted territory, there's Lily waiting to play wingman. No time has passed and we revert right back to our old antics. We were giddily escorted up to our beautiful suite with ornate details, and the second the butler left, we got naked, our suitcases exploding into total utter chaos. We can ruin a room in SECONDS. I promise you've never seen anything like it. Especially post-transition now that I have even more clothes and makeup than Lily does. Having Lily borrow my straightener or a dress gives me instant butterflies. I finally get to return the support she's given me all these years.

That first night, we decided to go out to the theater to see *Cabaret* followed by our favorite nightclub: the Box. Remember that club I rented on Day 365, earlier on in the book? Well, the Box has a British twin, and she's even naughtier than America's version. This wasn't my first time at London's Box, but it would be my first time visiting as a woman. I changed into an off-the-shoulder top and no pants, just pantyhose and black undies. I've gotten so good at tucking that there was no sign that MY box held family jewels.

I stood in the club line, in the pouring rain, not having contacted anyone to make a reservation (I always just hope that my smile will be currency). This was a particularly busy night, and some of the girls in line next to us recognized me. We continued to get shoved back and denied by the bouncer, who said we'd need to talk to someone named Ella. I was losing hope until the most gorgeous young blonde gal you've ever seen popped her head out. "Ella?" I yelled, not knowing if this was the HBIC. "Oh my god! Get in here!" the blonde yelled back.

Lily and I scurried in from the rain and were met with warmth from the blonde, who had just been barking orders at the bouncers. "Love! I watch your videos. You are so inspiring. Take my number down so if you ever want to come back we'll get you right in," she said with a smile. Another win for the blondes. Thanks, Ella! I looked back at the long line behind me. I wish I could've brought in every single girl wearing tiny dresses waiting in the rain outside. It's kind of like pet adoption, and Lily was the teacup Chihuahua I chose, but you can't bring every single one home. **Cue: Sarah McLachlan's "Angel."**

We danced our asses off. As the night continued and I peed a few times, my tuck wasn't quite as impressive at the end of the night. The great thing about a club like the Box is it's so dark I coulda had a large sofa attached to my crotch and no one would've noticed.

This was the first time I went out with Lily to a club where I actually felt as beautiful as she made me feel. I wasn't the gay best friend. I wasn't the pitied trans plus-one. I was now the OTHER hot blonde. The best part of being out with Lily is that she's both stunning AND married, so the hottest guys flock, but she isn't interested in the slightest. My only competition was with the other girls at the club. I marveled at the way they would give lap dances to business executives just to have a place to sit. A group of skinny rich boys from Spain started dancing with Lily and me. The hottest one, and the clear leader, grabbed my waist and started making small talk. Eeeee! We cooled off at the bar, and he offered to buy us drinks.

"What would you like?"

"Um, could I have a beer?"

"Wow."

"What?"

"You don't look like a beer drinker."

He had nooooo idea.

I handed Lily her tequila soda and gave her eyebrows, which she correctly interpreted as "go entertain the dweeby friend."

She was typically the one who got me a drink while I entertained the dweeby friend.

Just as the Spaniard was off settling the check, most likely with Daddy's money, I felt a hand around my waist. Uh-oh. I follow the hand up to the sexiest bicep, to the tightest sleeve of a black cotton shirt, to the strongest neck muscle, to the hunkiest jawline, to the dreamiest blue eyes staring back at me.

"You're the most stunning girl in the place."

End of book.

Dylan Mulvaney, 1996–2023.

Cause of death: hot man called her pretty.

As I began to say thank you, I felt a tap on my shoulder. It was the Spaniard holding my beer.

Ohhhhh shit.

The next scene was something out of a John Wayne movie. I don't really know who John Wayne is and I've never seen any of his movies, but I think he does Cowboy Westerns, and this was that.

A standoff.

The two men look at each other. Then me. Then each other. Then back to me.

And then the famous last words.

"Are you with him?" the tall stranger asks me.

I look at the Spanish nepo baby holding my beer. He's sweet. I've vetted him a bit.

I look at the tall stranger, whose hand hasn't left my waist.

I don't know his name, but I only know he finds me stunning. That's enough for me to respond:

"Um ... we're not together," I say with a half shameful look toward the Spaniard.

He looks broken. I feel my stomach drop. I'm a total bitch.

I look back at the tall stranger.

I'm a total bitch being held by a total ten.

"Have a good night, mate," the stranger says. I now clock his thick British accent.

The sad boy left my beer on the bar and retreated toward Lily and his dweeby friend. I was feeling horribly guilty until I remembered he was, in fact, a man, and this would be good for his ego in the long run. Lily hadn't watched the John Wayne movie unfold and was only catching the ending, looking at me like: "WHAT THE HELL IS HAPPENING?!"

I batted my eyelashes and gestured with my head to British sexy man and knew that she would take out the recycling.

"I'm Luke," he says with confidence, as he just won his pissing match.

"I'm Dyl," I respond. Who the fuck is Dyl?

Apparently Dyl is the total bitch who just traded one hot guy for a hotter one. I don't know where Dylan is right now. Oh that's right, she passed away on the last page.

"Wanna dance, Dyl?" he asks.

"Let's!" Dyl responds.

He firmly takes my hand, as if to make sure no other cowboy tries anything funny, as he leads me to the main room, dark, but less crowded as the night stretched on.

We start grinding on each other, making little bits of small talk.

I could tell he was posh, but his accent wasn't proper enough and his 2014 ripped skinny jeans were tipping me off that he wasn't a member of the royal family.

"I feel like I recognize you from something," he said.

"Oh, maybe!" Dyl responds.

"Are you an actress?" he asks.

"Yes, not sure if you'd recognize me, though." Unless he saw *The Book of Mormon* from 2019–2020 in America, he probably isn't familiar with my work.

"I was on TV a while back," he offers.

"What show?!"

"*Made in Chelsea*," he responds. I knew that was reality TV and could get very gossipy.

My British prince was actually a reality TV star, but hey, we both have our baggage.

I felt his dick press up against my booty, and there was very little fabric on my end separating me from virginity.

"Can I kiss you?" he asks.

I couldn't believe it. My first kiss as a girl, with someone THIS hot?! Take off the training wheels, Dyl, we're going straight for the gold. I looked at his face, coming closer to mine, almost as if it wasn't a question but rather a statement. I wanted to be selfish. I wanted this moment for the girl who had never gotten the jock growing up. For the girl who always entertained the dweeby friend. For the girl who never had two guys fighting over her. "Uh . . . I need to tell you something first," Dyl whispered.

DYL, WHAT THE FUCK ARE YOU DOING?!

"What's up?" he asked, genuinely interested and slightly confused, still holding me by the waist.

"Um . . . I'm trans."

He started laughing.

"Yeah right," he giggled.

I wish I was joking. If there was one moment I could let my transness melt away, and I could just be a woman for the next few minutes, without shame, loathing, anatomy, or baggage, it would be this one. But that's not really how this works, is it? As much as my life can feel like a fairy tale, when the clock strikes midnight, I'm still trans. Honesty is the best policy. Even in a posh crowded nightclub.

"Nope," I awkwardly said. This was Dylan talking, Dyl was long gone. His grip on me loosened.

"Oh, damn," he replied. "I had no idea . . . You're telling me you were a guy before?" he asked with a squint in his eye, as if he squinted hard enough he would see the man I once cosplayed.

"I transitioned last year," I said matter-of-factly.

"Only a year ago? DAMN," he said.

I scanned every word for some sign, some direction on how he felt.

"Have you ever been with a trans woman?" I asked.

"Never," he replied quickly.

Eeek.

"I think I need to take a minute if that's okay and have a think," he said after moments of silence.

"Google trans beer girl while you're at it," I word vomit.

WHAT ARE YOU DOING NOW?! IF THERE WAS ANY CHANCE OF HIM LIKING YOU, YOU JUST OBLITERATED THAT.

But seriously, why did I say that?

Subconsciously, I knew that my baggage was bigger than his reality show past. That my transness was a heavy lift, especially for a straight man who didn't have experience with a girl like me. And that maybe my fame and controversy was actually heavier baggage than my transness is. So I put it all out there for him. If he was chill with all of it, I'd get to kiss him without shame.

"I'll just be a minute," he says, as he walks away. Lily, on red alert this entire interaction, flocks to me like a mama bird whose baby just fell hard.

"What the hell is going on?" she asks.

I fill her in. She turns to comfort me and tries to read my emotions. Lily holds her breath, sensing I'm about to cry before I do, but I don't feel the tears tonight, I feel pride for how I handled that. She exhales.

Lily and I shift our eyes to the corner of the club, where Luke is now sitting in a booth, hunched over his bright phone screen with the hyperfocus of a college kid on Adderall.

"He's googling Beergate," I say to Lily.

HAHAHAHAHHAHA, we burst out cackling.

"How the fuck did we get here!!!" Lily lets out. We've been asking ourselves that a lot lately.

Luke returns to where I'm standing on the dance floor, and Lily slyly exits.

"Hi," he says.

"Hi," I say.

He pulls out his phone.

"So you're telling me this is YOU?" He shows me a screengrab of myself in a *Daily Mail* article.

"Yep!" I say.

"You are WAY hotter in person," he says.

I exhale.

"Did you have . . . the surgery?" he asks.

"Not yet."

"Alright. Alright," he says. "I think I'm cool with it."

DYL RE-ENTERS THE CHAT, IT'S A BRITISH MIRACLE!

Just as we draw closer to each other, I feel his hand grab mine, but his gaze was now drifting across the room.

"So, tell me about your friend that you're here with," he says.

I spot Lily waiting for me a few feet away.

"That's my best friend Lily. We've known each other since we were ten."

"Would she be down to join?" he asks.

My heart sinks. Oh.

"She's married," I say coldly.

"Married . . . or *married*-married?" he asks, with a slight laugh. Ick.

"Married. Married."

I could tell this was no longer the hot fantasy I had built up in my head. I had gone from the prizewinning show pony to the old horse that they were about to put out to pasture. The bar was clearing out. 3:47 a.m. I could tell Lily was tired. So was I.

"You can meet me at my flat later, I might meet up with some mates first," he offers.

How romantic.

"I'm gonna get Lily home."

He leans for a kiss. I offer my cheek. We awkwardly hug. I give him my number. Lily and I get in the Uber.

"You okay, Dyl?" Lily asks.

"It's Dylan now, and yeah, I think so." I didn't have much to compare this to, so I was genuinely trying to decipher if I was happy or sad about the interaction. Lily and I climbed into the giant plush king-sized hotel bed.

"Can we get an order of fries, a BLT, a kids' mac and cheese, and a scoop of vanilla ice cream?" Lily asks the room service operator, our go-to order.

I wash off the makeup, see the stubble growing back in, and think about waking up in that guy's random apartment in the morning. How I'd need to dry shave using his razor before he notices. Is this what I'm signing up for going forward? When do I stop needing to come out?

When will I be enough for one person?

There *was* comfort in non-passing. There was comfort in walking into a room with my transness one step ahead of me. There was comfort being the funny friend who entertains the dweeb.

I crawl into bed with Lily, who sets up our room service on top of the duvet.

A piece of mac and cheese falls onto the white sheets from my fork.

I eat it. There's a small yellow stain.

Moments later, I'm soundly asleep on top of that yellow stain. Another sleep as a girl who hasn't had her first kiss.

* * * * *

The next morning, I wake up jet-lagged and hungover. Lily called for coffee.

"I'm taking you to the women's pond today," she says.

Lily had told me many times about the women's pond, a natural swimming hole in a large park called Hampstead Heath, where women swim with their friends at all times of the year. I was nervous, knowing it was strictly a women-only space, and I wasn't sure how they'd feel about a trans gal, but Lily assured me I could wear my swimsuit. I tucked and caked on makeup, ready for the day.

Hampstead Heath was like . . . storybook cute. Is everything outside of America automatically a thousand times more charming?! Central Park had nothing on her. I skipped along the paths, a blonde in a white dress who had somewhere to get to.

Lily and I walked up to the women's pond, paid our admission, and in the dressing area I pulled out a surprise.

"Please," I beg as I hand Lily a bright blue swim cap with flowers all over it. I put mine on.

She obliges. We wait our turn for the swim ladder and wade in. It's deep! Lily and I hold on to each other as we doggy paddle to one of the flotation rings in the middle of the pond. Women swim around us, no one gives me a second look. Just gals all trying to stay afloat.

We shower, then find a little hill to sunbathe and dry off. Nearby, a fox grabs a lady's sandwich right off her towel.

Lily begins her lesson plan. "I think you need to navigate straight men differently."

"You can't ask a ton of questions. Let them drive the conversation. Otherwise, they'll get spooked."

Ugh. This will kill me. I love driving a convo.

"So, I'm guessing I shouldn't open with 'Are you happy?'" My go-to ice breaker.

"DEFINITELY not."

Lily and I went on to practice my "eyes across the bar" face followed by a new feminine laugh. At one point, she sat up with a revelation.

"And no kissing bandit," she stressed. This unlocked a core memory: my habit of serial kissing boys at parties as a teen. I think I was so willing to kiss as many men as possible in a single eve because it felt like a game. For every time I told myself I was unworthy of love, a kiss from a new boy was a strike against that belief. I didn't want to repeat that behavior this time around.

"You need to make them work for it. Try to not kiss them upon meeting if you think there's a future there. Unless it's for sure just a hookup." I knew this would be difficult for me, since I once assumed that if I don't put out right away, they'll find someone that will. That my body would bring them to me and my killer personality would make them stay. Maybe I try Lily's way.

The next morning, Lily and I said goodbye, really not knowing the next time we'd see each other. Breaks my heart every time. The day I left was day 499 of girlhood. I listened to Billie Eilish's "What Was I Made For?" over and over again on the Uber to the airport. I filmed a vid, looking at the camera with the text "Day 500 tomorrow" as the sad song played in the background. It gets a million likes. At the ticket counter, the agent studied my male passport, lets out an exaggerated gasp, "Oh!"

Fuck.

"Dylan Mulvaney! Wow! We're delighted to have you here with us!"

Sweet!

* * * * *

"Hi, ladies!" Liza yelled from a lounge chair next to the pool. Sabrina and I arrived together, then made the hour-and-a-half drive to Antibes, a small coastal town in France that was known for its art, beach clubs, and sixteenth-century architecture. The house was even bigger and more magnificent than the listing Liza sent. Plus, we each had our own bedroom. This was different from my previous vacations with friends, where we'd all cram into one room and have to sneak in because we'd be over capacity. Liza's gorgeous costume designer friend Mia rounded out the group to an even four, and we connected instantly over our love of vintage, retro clothing. Our first night, the four of us walked the old town and found a cute bar for happy hour.

I looked around at the other outside tables. Three out of four were smoking cigarettes and looked damn good doing it. Uh-oh. My vice.

"Do we dare?" said one of the girls, noticing my stare.

"I'll go get some!" I hopped up before she could get the words out.

"Make sure you get the skinny ones!"

A few steps away at a nearby convenience store, I stared up at the rows and rows of cigarettes, all of them covered in photos of rotting lungs and X-rays. Woof.

"Skinny?" I asked.

The associate looked at me funny.

"Petite?" I pointed to my pinky.

He grabbed a long box. I payed and then opened. Jackpot!

I lit up and we cosplayed as sexy French supermodels. We slurped oysters and flirted with the French waiter who was flirting right back.

"Okay, this is a slight change of plans, but how do we feel about going on a yacht in Saint-Tropez tomorrow?" Liza asked the group.

Was this my new hot girl normal?

We all giddily agree. "Pack an overnight bag!" Liza urged when we arrived back home.

I woke up extra early so I could film a Day 500 video. It was the first *Days of Girlhood* video I'd made since Beergate, and it was long, and serious, and filled with all the things I had learned. The girls and I piled into the back of a minivan and made the two-hour drive north to Saint-Tropez. A German man yelled at us to hurry on arrival, and we hopped into the boat. "WOW! This is great!" I exclaimed.

"This is the dinghy," said the German man.

The boat to take us to the bigger boat. Got it.

We climbed onto the giant yacht and immediately started kissing cheeks. There were four husbands and four wives. Liza had met one of the couples at an event and now they met up on spontaneous vacation moments like this. Now that I am hot and blonde, I wonder if I too will have access to yachts. Keep ya updated.

I sat down next to Sabrina at the lunch table, where a giant spread of every kind of appetizer lay in front of us, with nearly a dozen staff buzzing around pouring rosé and offering bread. Our host raised a glass: "To new friends!"

"To new friends!" we cheered.

I was feeling confident and pretty, but on guard. Once upon a time I would've tried to impress people this wealthy, but now I have enough self-worth to feel like their money can't buy my praise.

"So, Dylan." The host looked in my direction.

"You remind me of my brother," he said with zero hesitation in his German accent.

I felt Sabrina's eyes dart toward me. Everyone's eyes darted toward me.

"And why is that?" I asked him.

"He now wants to go by 'she.' He is keeping his name like you," he said.

At this point, Sabrina had grabbed my hand under the table, Liza was channeling some mama bird energy, and I could tell the girls would be ready to jump overboard if I gave the order. I didn't feel like running away, but I did feel like I was backed into a corner. The confidence that the blonde had given me drained out of my body, and the hours of effort, the fake lashes, the tuck, the higher pitch of my voice, none of it mattered anymore. He got me.

"Well, I think SHE sounds amazing. Tell me more about HER," I responded. And he proceeded to do exactly as I'd instructed.

He recounted their childhood, the way that he constantly had to fight off her bullies, and her present-day aversion to connecting with other trans people. He didn't understand why she wouldn't try to find community.

"I think some trans people are nervous about connection with others like them because it can bring out a lot of shared trauma. She also might not want to bring attention to her transness and wishes to just live her life as a woman. Either way, if she ever does want a gal pal to chat with, please pass along my info to her," I said.

Everyone watched this convo like Wimbledon. Play ball. Does that saying apply to tennis? I digress.

"But what about the people letting their kids transition in the States, it is so unsafe and corrupt," one of the wives interjected. Clearly, I had made the rest of the table feel like they could serve it up, so if Professor Dylan needed to make a summer school appearance, class was in session.

"The information you have seems to be very skewed, and I'd be interested to know where you've heard those things. Access to gender-affirming care for children is extremely difficult to come by, and . . ." I didn't stop for a good ten minutes. I talked about my family, my faith, my trans friends, my euphoria, my dysphoria, my dark thoughts, my hopes and dreams for the community. We're gonna have to ask one of the girls, but I'm pretty sure I stood up at one point. The only thing I knew was that these men and women had extreme amounts of privilege, and besides his trans sister, I might be the only exposure to transness that these folks would ever have. I was visibly passionate. I didn't want to have to be a teacher on vacation, but I was happily surprised by the numerous facts I was able to offer. The strength I had cultivated to protect myself was now enough to protect others. At the end of my speech (or tirade), the table started to let out a little applause.

"Thank you for that," the host said. "You obviously have much care in your heart." He smiled at me with a cheeky smirk, as if my hazing was over. I didn't know if I wanted to punch him or fuck him.

"I'm so proud of you," Sabrina whispered.

"I think I blacked out," I whispered back.

The host then moved on to global warming, after which he discussed Russia's invasion of Ukraine, followed by a rant on Brexit. Most of their views on the subjects were quite liberal, I noticed. So, it seemed like transness was just one of the courses. I sat pretty quiet for the others.

After lunch, tensions eased and everyone was happily tipsy.

At this point, the nanny brought out their children, who I didn't even know were present on the ship, and the kids started jumping off the boat (by choice, and not because of painful lunch conversations). I decided to jump too.

It was cuckoo high. I don't know WHY I refused to take off my jewelry for my jump (probably for the photo op), but I lost a pearl earring my dad got me from Tiffany's last Christmas. Dylan, there are people who are dying.

Toward the end of the day, the billionaires and co. all warmed up to us once they learned of our awards and accomplishments. I think rich people want to be famous, and famous people want to be rich. That's why we're all on this boat, isn't it?

* * * * *

As we headed toward shore, the host turned to us and said, "We have reserved a table at the best beach club tonight for dancing and party. We will send you to our home on land to freshen up and will send a car to fetch you. The house is yours for the weekend." (He sounded like a bond villain instructing us on our own demise, which obviously made me more excited to check out this "house" that was "ours" for the weekend.)

The house was mammoth, with a Vegas hotel–sized swimming pool that was giving water park vibes. I was waiting for the waves to start up. After my harrowing almost-hookup in London, I wanted to take a fresh approach to a night out. I rinsed off the ocean water, straightened my salty hair, put on my tiniest blue tube top, a white skirt, and blue beads, and glued pearls all over my eyes. I looked young. I looked like a cast member from an equity touring production of *Mamma Mia!* The girls and I gathered in the foyer, and they looked EQUALLY fire. I have a hard time understanding why certain hot women don't thrive around other hot women. It makes me feel even more powerful and cute.

The beach club was on the sand, with a rope stopping you from going toward the water and security blocking off the ocean. It's as if they knew about my 2012 Fourth of July skinny-dipping escapade. (I ran away from my friends to collect shells in a sock. They eventually found me, heavy sock in hand, nakedly flailing around the ocean.) I made a promise to myself that tonight wouldn't be a repeat offense. When I get drunk, I do love to go off by myself, and I do love to find a body of water. Not my proudest quality, Lily would agree.

The club was packed with hotties crowding around tables scattered on a platform in the sand. I was on my best behavior as we sat at our table with the couples from the yacht, and they treated us like old friends. They were in their forties, but I could tell that they wanted to blow off some steam. Three hours into the meal, the waitstaff pulled all the tables and chairs away and the entire place turned into a dance floor. I swear to God Satan himself came down and implanted himself into the dick of every man in that club, because I had never experienced the amount of chaos that ensued on that dance floor. I can only describe it as an episode of *The Bachelorette.*

I stood in one spot, on a step slightly above the dancing area, and the men lined up to greet me. They would say their name, where they were from, grab my waist, ask me to dance. I would say, "Maybe later," and then they would fade into the crowd defeated. I kept looking back at the girls to make sure this was actually real life and I hadn't hit my head on a table when they were moving them out of the way. Mia played backup, and if two guys approached me simultaneously, we'd watch them decide which one wanted me and which one wanted her. I loved watching them use their boy math to figure out the answer based on height, age, and personality type. One pair actually switched mid convo with us without even acknowledging each other, they just knew.

The yacht husbands and wives were getting the show of their lives—watching me fight off the men. The yacht's owner even came to dance with me at one point, holding my hand and grinding on me. Sick fuck. I loved it.

"We're heading to a house party," one of the wives yelled to us, and I followed the group out, looking back at all my prospects. Oh well.

I kid you not, this house was giving . . . Versailles big. Like so nice they don't even show it on Zillow vibes. But it was also giving . . . *murder*. Whenever I'm around really rich people I feel like I'm about to be given sixty seconds to run into the woods until they start hunting me lol. The party was filled with all sorts of rich men and hot girls, and it was definitely the witching hour. I went to flirt with a guy or two just to have a supermodel hiss "get away from my man" at me in a Russian accent. These women felt like pre-professional billionaire wives, not with the rings yet, but close. There I was in my Spandex bandeau and plastic pearls falling off my eyelids. I couldn't compete. To make matters worse, Sabrina and I were starving. We saw people eating burgers and fries coming from the kitchen. We headed straight for the goods and knocked on the door.

"Yes?" a man in a chef's hat said.

"Hi, could we get some food please?" I smiled. I could see multiple people cooking behind him.

"Not for you," he barked and slammed the door shut.

"Huh?" Sabrina said.

Seconds later, we watch a couple knock, and the chef handed them two burgers and a massive plate of fries. You're kidding.

We knocked again.

"Hi, is the food coming out later? We saw them just . . ."

Another "Not enough for you" and door slam in our faces.

"SHE HAS AN OSCAR!" I yell through the door. Sabrina shoots me a glare, but then we laugh.

Not even an Oscar is currency on billionaire island. We all decided to head back to the house, with no kisses, and no burgers. After a few more days of debauchery (with a special guest appearance by Lily, guess the dramatic goodbye wasn't necessary), I headed back to LA to put my new flirting skills to the test back home.

* * * * *

The day after I got back to Los Angeles, I found myself three dirty Shirley Temples deep at a Power of Young Hollywood event. So much for Woo-Woo Dylan's healing, Party Dylan was on overtime. Mid-event, I was tapped on the shoulder.

"Dylan?"

"Hi, love! How are you?" came my canned response to the sweet young girl who approached me.

"It's Josie," she said bluntly.

I racked my brain. Josie . . . Josie . . . Josie . . . actress and trans icon JOSIE TOTAH? I take in her tiny petite frame, high voice, and stunningly soft features.

"BITCH! YOU'RE TRANS?" I scream.

"BITCH, YES!" We embrace.

It's moments like these I'm reminded how good those prepuberty 'mones hit. Damn, I wish.

We agree to leave the party early and head to a dive bar, Good Times at Davey Wayne's. I hadn't been there in years, but I remembered entering through a fridge and really good music.

I had recruited a small group of queers from the party to join us. Alok, our friend Colton Haynes, and Josie, whom I'd just met, all watched as I slowly started dancing with a hot guy. With his pale skin and dark hair, he looked like a vampire (my type!). As we dance, I find out he's Romanian and likes to ride motorcycles. Then, out of nowhere, he leans in to kiss me. I . . . ran . . . to the bathroom.

Josie followed me in.

"What are you doing?!" Josie confronts me.

I was already tearing up. A little drunk.

"I still haven't been kissed and what if he doesn't know I'm trans I'm so tired of coming out over and over and . . ." All the words came out of my mouth, and I couldn't stop them.

"OH FOR CHRIST SAKES YOU DON'T HAVE TO FUCK THE GUY—JUST KISS HIM!!" she yells.

"I don't have to come out to him beforehand?"

"No, he should be so lucky to make out with you! Now go!"

I exited the bathroom and the Romanian vampire man was still on the dance floor, waiting for me. ABBA's "Take a Chance on Me" exploded over the speakers.

I walked up and tried to pick back up where I awkwardly left off. We swayed. We smiled. He leaned . . . I leaned . . . and . . .

BOOM. KISS. WE DID IT, DYL.

As our lips connected, I heard cheers from across the floor. Josie and friends were screaming as they watched the entire moment unfold. My man looked confused by them but continued kissing me. We exchanged numbers, and he wanted to take me home. But I knew that was enough excitement for one night. I left the bar buzzing. The sex witch's curse is broken! Josie and I—instant friends for life—made plans to hang out all weekend. Alok and I headed to my place to replay the moment over and over again until we fell asleep.

I texted with vampire man throughout the weekend, and he finally invited me out on a proper date. I hadn't told him I was trans, and this particular evening I was having dinner with a group of trans and queer folks. My coming-out text was the main topic of dinner discussion.

"Believe me, you need to tell him now and not in person. I've been in this situation a million times," said L'lerrét, Alok's friend I'd just met that night.

We craft the text.

"Hi, I'm really looking forward to getting together soon, but wanted you to know that I'm trans."

I really wanted to add a "hope that's okay," but the table demanded I resist. I sent the text and dropped my phone on the table.

We all waited for the reply. Dots. Moments later:

"I feel like you were tricking me," he sends back. He continues on to say that he's upset. Everyone at the table instantly chimed in with "fuck him" and various fighting words. I was feeling the sadness seep in. Nope nope nope.

"Let's go." I stood up from the table.

"Where?" Alok asked me.

"Dancing," I said.

Within twelve minutes of receiving that text, I was back on the dance floor at Davey Wayne's, this time a different ABBA song playing. The only option to cure my sadness was to quickly make sure he wasn't my one and only kiss for a second longer. I pointed at a tall guy with long hair and curled my finger toward me. He followed my summon. By the next song, I was making out with a French creative director and my friends' jaws were on the floor. NEXT!

I left, not giving him my number. I didn't feel all that sad. I felt realistic. I had a better sense of the terrain ahead. I knew that I didn't owe men my identity from the get-go, but if things were going to move farther south, I would need to divulge the bulge. I needed to protect myself.

Still, every other night for the next few months, I would walk through the Davey Wayne's fridge, point to the hottest guy on the dance floor, and we'd eat each other's faces. It was like clockwork, a game for me. I picked up on their pick-up lines: "You look like Margot Robbie." "You're the hottest girl here." "I love blondes." I was doing what Lily told me not to do—but these weren't datable men. They were warm bodies there to prove something to my shadow self. I would never go home with any of them, always leaving the bar alone. I'd get in bed smug, but as the months passed and my kissing numbers hit double digits, I felt sad that I was being so aimless. I'm so specific and thoughtful in every other area of my life, why not try that in love too? I haven't visited Davey Wayne's dance floor much recently, so I haven't been getting much action. But I did get my tits sucked after an awards show, and that felt awesome.

Colby, my psychic, has proclaimed that this year is the year I find love, so I can relax a little and not chase. The "once I's" that I would refer to for finding love have begun to fade and turn into something else. "Once I get bottom surgery" is now "once I stop hurting myself." "Once I get rid of my beard" became "once I love myself." I am starting to believe that there is nothing I need to gain or strip away in order to find love, except for seeing the value within me. The same value that my friends, family, and followers see every day. And if all else fails, I'll always have Lily for BFF sleepovers on a bed of mac and cheese crumbs to keep me warm.

DAY 293 of being a girl . . .

. . . And it's my first birthday as a girl. Today I got my nose cast off and I was not thrilled with the result. "You look so beautiful!" the few friends I've invited over for a reveal tell me. NO I DON'T, BITCH! So while I wait for the swelling to go down and my face to look human again, why don't I run down some highlights from my birthdays past.

Ninth birthday: Knott's Berry Farm. My parents were actively getting a divorce, and since they were in the same place, I spent the whole day trying to determine if they would get back together or not.

Tenth birthday: Disneyland on December 29 is hell. Park was at full capacity. My sister Stacey got to bring a friend and I didn't. Three-hour ride lines. Not ideal.

Twelfth birthday: Saw *Wicked* the musical in LA and got to go backstage with the cast. Met with a talent agent afterward. Mom let me sit in the front seat of the car for the first time.

Fourteenth birthday: Saw the musical *Next to Normal* in LA with two friends and my mom. I demanded we go to the Ivy because I googled restaurants where celebs go, and it popped up. It was so expensive that we had to split the ravioli and we each got one raviolo.

Fifteenth birthday: Made my dad take my family and me to the Melting Pot, a fondue restaurant. He HATES fondue. SO expensive and you have to cook your own dinner. I'm obsessed.

Sixteenth birthday: Mom got me a stretch limo off Groupon from 3 to 5 p.m. on a Saturday. Lily was the only friend who showed up. I wanted to get my cartilage pierced, but my mom said she'd disown me. We blasted Enya and cried. Limo driver took us to get gelato.

Eighteenth birthday: House party at my dad's. Everyone kissed me at midnight. El Chapo's family showed up. The neighbor Lily and I both hooked up with got into a fistfight with Curly from the local production of *Oklahoma!*

Nineteenth birthday: Party bus to a strip club. Made friends with a stripper named Daisy and deserted my friends to go to a bar with her. We smoked cigs on a curb. Brought hot Australians back to my house in the party bus, but they promptly left when they found out I had a cat (deathly allergic).

Twenty-first birthday: Vegas, duh! My friends and I sold our nudes to buy Britney Spears tickets off Craigslist an hour before to discover that it was an underground counterfeit ticket ring the

venue ushers were running. Stood front row—
got vocal nodes from screaming. Lily got carried
out of a club by bouncers kicking and screaming
after attempting to get behind the DJ booth.

Twenty-fifth birthday: Wine tasting in Napa Valley
with Lily. Horseback riding and then four vineyards.
Got blackout drunk, woke up next day with alcohol
poisoning AND Covid, then drove twelve hours home.

Twenty-sixth birthday: Got my nose cast off and the
screws taken out of my head. Got a limo for Lily, Keesh,
and me. Went to Burberry and bought a checkered skirt
and jacket set, my dream outfit since I was little. In
the spirit of my first birthday as a girl, I hired a mini
pony to keep me company.

One-year-old Dylan got the pony she always wanted, and
twenty-six-year-old Dylan got the nose job she always
wanted. And no strippers or fistfights in sight. This
must be adulthood.

LOVE YA,

Dylan♥

DAY 356 of being a girl . . .

. . . And today I am moving into the Plaza Hotel in New York City. When people would ask me what I wanted to be when I grew up, I would say a concierge at the Plaza. Their reactions were usually a little confused because it came from a five-year-old. My response was partly because *Eloise at the Plaza* was my favorite movie, but really it stemmed from my obsession with hospitality. Since I can remember, I've always jumped at

the opportunity to research the best restaurants, find the cheapest flights, and recommend Broadway shows.

The few trips I got to go to New York as a kid, I always made sure to walk by the Plaza and daydream about what it would be like to run the halls like Eloise. Today, that changes.

When I started planning for Day 365 of girlhood, my imagination and expectations knew no limits. I had already settled on the big day being a musical evening in New York City and landed on the Rainbow Room in Midtown Manhattan.

I would need a place to stay while rehearsing the show in the Big Apple. Since I was on my longest streak of luck, I wanted to take one last gamble and set my eyes on the Plaza. When their marketing team emailed me back with open arms, five-year-old concierge Dylan let out an earth-shattering scream. "Lily, pack your bags! WE GOT THE PLAZA." I hired Lily to be my wrangler, which meant a month-long sleepover. Lily's other duties included setting up the humidifiers for my voice, ordering room service, and, most of all, managing my frequent panic attacks.

The concierge Daniel showed us up to our room— they put us directly across from the special Eloise suite. I packed a full Eloise costume in hopes that they'd let me film in there sometime during my stay. As soon as Daniel left us, Lily and I let out a squeal, put on robes, and jumped on the bed.

I only had a few minutes before glam arrived in prep
for presenting at the PFLAG gala that evening. We
nibbled on the scones the hotel had left for us and
tickled each other's arms.

A Conversation with Lily

Me: I wonder if this is what my life is going to be like
from now on. Or if it's all just gonna come to an end.

Lily: What do you mean?

Me: Like, what if this is the peak of my life
and I'll never stay at the Plaza ever again?

Lily: You'll definitely stay at the Plaza again.

She hops up and I hear her start the tub faucet.
Speed bath. Good idea.

We giggle in the tub until Laurel and Zenobia,
my glam team and fellow dolls, arrive.

"Girl look at us!" Laurel exclaims as we hug for
the first time in months. She was the first person to
professionally do my makeup, two years ago when I was
nonbinary, at the start of both of our careers. Now she
does Doja Cat and Melanie Martinez, and has kept me on
even though she's soaring. Zenobia is a drag artist and
queen of all things hair, who Laurel recommended. I had
them booked nearly every day until showtime because
of all the press, events, and promo I was set to do. The
three of us trans girls and Lily all getting ready in a

Plaza suite felt like the highest high. I bicker with my stylist Brad Goreski over text; he doesn't want to let me do a braid crown to pair with my Stella McCartney gladiator dress because he told me it would look too costume-y. I win the text fight. Zenobia proceeds with the braid crown. Lily and I take photos on the Plaza steps before hopping into our car. At the gala, Lily and I try to decide if we want to go somewhere else after. "We got the Plaza," I tell her. She immediately understands. We head home. I start rehearsal for my show tomorrow. Lily waits for me in bed. We rent *Eloise* the movie, since Lily has never seen it. She always falls asleep before me, usually twenty minutes into the movie. I look up at the high ceiling and think about God. This is one of the most solid things God has ever done for me. I'm so happy.

LOVE YA,

Dylan♥

DAY 364 of being a girl . . .

. . . And Mamma Mia, here we go again. I've been
rehearsing my Day 365 show for a week. It's somehow
all coming together. Don't get me wrong, I've sobbed
a few times and have taken my fair share of ADHD
meds, but there's a chance I might just pull it off
tomorrow. We've run through the show twice, and everything goes great until . . . the Sondheim medley.

If you don't know who Stephen Sondheim was, I am
worried about you. He's one of musical theater's
greatest composers of all time. For my big eleven
o'clock number, I selected three of his tunes to put
into a medley. I chose "Not While I'm Around" from
Sweeney Todd, followed by "Children Will Listen"
and "No One Is Alone," both from *Into the Woods*. The
songs were framed around supporting the Trevor
Project, an organization that provides crisis services
to LGBTQ+ youth. I wanted the kids watching the
livestream to know that they aren't alone, and the
parents watching to realize just how crucial
their acceptance of their children's identity
expressions is.

I get through the first song just fine, and then I
start the monologue before "Children Will Listen":

"If there are parents watching, major props to you. I am honored that you trust me enough to be a character in your children's lives. I came out to my mom as a girl when I was four years old and 8,107 days later we are now just celebrating my first year of girlhood." (This is where I start sobbing.) "If that tells you anything, it's that kids are a lot smarter than we think they are." (Snot running down my nose.) "And if you do have a queer child, just know that you have the power to change their trajectory, for better or for worse." (The words have become inaudible and I sound more like a howler monkey that stubbed its toe.) "Your words have more power than you could ever imagine."

By the time I was supposed to begin singing, everyone in the rehearsal room knew that I couldn't. The piano dropped out, and over the past two days I would wave off the director to give me a second. All of the dramatics were because I referenced my mom. It had been nearly six months since we'd spoken and it was killing me inside knowing that she wouldn't be at the show the next evening. The only communication we had was a few weeks before when I texted her to invite her to Day 365, and she texted back that her husband's brother would be visiting that week so she couldn't attend. I knew that if I tried to sing that song tomorrow without speaking to her beforehand, it would be a meltdown just like today, but this time in front of thousands of people.

"Are you going to be able to get through it tomorrow?" asks Alyah, who agreed to produce the show.

"Yeah. I just need to call her tonight. I'm gonna do it."

"You're SURE that's a good idea, opening up that wound the night before the show?" she adds.

"Yep. I need to." I am wildly confident in my decision.

I got back to the Plaza and Lily hung out in the lobby so I'd have the room to myself for the phone call. The past few months without reaching out to her were painful. Mom's approval has always been my addiction, and if me calling her tonight is considered a relapse, then so be it.

The first ring.

A thought hits me: *What if SHE doesn't want to talk to ME? What if this call wasn't fair to HER?* I had heard from my dad and sister that she asks about me frequently, so that brought me a bit of reassurance, but still I was—second ring.

A Conversation with My Mom

Mom: Hello?

Me: Hi, Mom!

Mom: Dylan, hi! How are you?

Me: I'm good. Just finished rehearsal for my show tomorrow.

Mom: The family is going to stream it live at Brett's house, we're all very excited.

Me: Aw! That makes me happy. How have you been?

We caught each other up on the past few months, as if no time had passed. It was oddly casual. After fifteen minutes of fluff, I said:

Me: I want to thank you for giving me space. I'm sorry that it hurt you.

Mom: No, no, I want to apologize. I've been seeing a counselor for a while now, and I've realized that I can't live without you in my life. I've felt like a piece of my heart is missing. I am team Dylan. I am your number one fan. I've prayed on this for a long time now, and God wouldn't want me to turn away from you. God knows what's in my heart. And I will be judged when the time comes.

I could hear her getting choked up, not unlike me during my rehearsal today. The pain was real for both of us, but for the first time in months, the tears were also healing. I didn't think I had any left in me, but sure enough, I could taste their saltiness on the corners of my smile.

"I love you. I don't want to get into anything too deep, but I'll call you soon. Wish you were here," I told her before getting off the phone.

"I wish I were too," she said.

I hung up knowing that I could get through the show tomorrow night.

Lily came back up and we got into bed.

"How'd that go?" she asked.

"We're gonna be okay."

LOVE YA,

Dylan♥

DAY 365 of being a girl . . .

. . . And it's going to be the best day ever. I turned my shower on to get the bathroom steamy for my singing voice, but the steroid I took feels like it's doing its job. Lily lags in the bed for a moment before joining me.

A Conversation with Lily

Lily: Heyyy.

Me: Heyyyyyy.

Lily: Happy 365. How do you feel?

Me: Ready for a cocktail.

Twelve hours until my big show at the Rainbow Room and a thousand things to get done. I need to post something, so I do an unboxing of the Chanel bag I bought myself as my big "you made it" gift. It's pink and wayyyy too expensive, but if there were ever a Treat Yourself Day, it's today. I keep reminding myself to enjoy this all while it lasts, and not worry about the fear of it all slipping away. Inevitably, things will ebb and flow, so how sucky would it be if I didn't live in these magical moments while I'm in the middle of having them?

I race to the Rainbow Room without a stitch of makeup, since I'll be glamming closer to the show.

We only have one run-through before the audience arrives. I've been so busy making all the other plates spin that as the run-through starts, I realize that I don't actually know if I memorized all of my lines. I might need to cash in on one of my God wishes. I think I've already used one or two.

We start and stop for lighting issues, orchestra tweaks, costume mishaps, but miraculously, I sort of know what I'm doing. I look around the room, where a hundred workers all buzz about, setting up chairs and hanging curtains. *Dylan!! This is all for you!!! Can you believe it?* I can't, actually. I always thought I'd exist in the ensemble, a boy trying to find full potential, but now I was the girl at center stage. Funny how finding your identity can kick that potential into high gear.

My special guests all showed up for their run-through time slots:

Dominique Jackson mothered me.

Jonathan Van Ness didn't know their lines but made me cackle.

Sis and L Morgan Lee lent me their Broadway talent.

Reneé Rapp comforted me in a duet.

This might be a real show! We didn't have time to get through the full run, but I figured the closing number can be blackout wildness. When in doubt, just pony in place! They whisked me down to the "red carpet," which was, naturally, pink. I hadn't had my hand in any of this part, so seeing my giant face on the step and repeat was probably the highlight of my life. There were many photographers, and I didn't move much because I was in my Christian Siriano gown, a giant cupcake. So, I just smiled and threw my hands up. It all sort of felt like a sweet sixteen, except I didn't have braces and my parents weren't paying for it.

Five minutes to places, and I start filming a makeup ad. "Are you seriously doing that right now?!" gasped Lily. "I have to," I tell her.

"Places, baby, places!" erupts Alyah.

I wait at the top of the staircase for my entrance music. So many important people in that room. Don't fuck it up. *They all want you to win.* As the music swells and the show begins, I hold for my first solo standing ovation ever. Little Dylan would've been giddy. The audience finally settles, but the energy is NEXT LEVEL. I hit every single mark. Nail almost every note. Get every line out. As the show progressed, I stopped repeatedly shocking myself and settled into the fact that this was actually happening. All of the moments, even the bad, were worth this single hour of bliss. When we got to the Sondheim medley, tears rolled down my face, not of sadness but of relief that my mom was back in my life. As I was pulling myself together, a very unexpected cameo was made. My dad had rushed the stage from the audience to comfort me. At first I was shocked and nearly annoyed, but when he hugged me I realized both he and I needed it. Definitely one of my favorite moments. One of my last lines, "Maybe this is like Day 1 of womanhood," felt more honest than when I originally wrote it. I made it through this chapter of girlhood, and now I can make it through whatever womanhood has in store. I can't wait to find out what that is.

LOVE YA,

Dylan ♥

P.S. LOVE YA

It's 12:40 p.m. on a Monday afternoon.

I'm sitting outside on the porch of my dream house that is currently out of my budget, in a tie-dye cotton dress with no tears or cigarettes in sight. My beard is growing in for an electrolysis session on Wednesday. I haven't received a single work email or text. My blonde hair is dry and dead, but my roots are growing in strong. I ate food this morning! I made my bed. The sheets could use a wash, but maybe tomorrow. Keesh is in town and is coming over for our favorite sushi takeout tonight. Lily is coming too.

As I grew closer to finishing this book, I didn't know what the stopping point would be. I had hoped for some sort of epic win, maybe my first big acting role on TV or losing my virginity as a girl as one last climax with you. But those things haven't happened yet. Also, I'm a little tired of eventful chaos, no matter how good or bad it is.

So how about we wrap this up during a rare occasion when the dark thoughts are at bay and I have a few cute wins? Would that be okay?

I've been trying things a little differently these past few weeks. I'm going back to the basics.

Last week I did my first stand-up comedy show since beginning *Days of Girlhood*. I opened for Alok's show in Salt Lake City. Being back up on that small stage, in front of a crowd of tangible people, felt like I was coming home. The biggest difference between stand-up pre-TikTok fame and now is that I already have the audience on my side. Back in 2021, when I was driving around LA trying to get five-minute spots, I felt like the audience was expecting me to be terrible, or at the least easily forgettable. Getting back up on that stand-up stage in my current form made me realize that comedians who do it without viral fame deserve their damn roses. I took the other route, and the laughs might be a little cheaper and easier to come by, but the fear of failure intensifies. Now if I bomb it won't just be "God, we saw this horrible comedian bomb tonight," it will be "God, we saw Dylan Mulvaney bomb tonight."

Luckily, that wasn't the case this time. A good majority of my set was around Beergate, the conservative politicians who love to hate me, and my likelihood to join a cult. As I spun the trauma of last summer into carefully crafted puns, the laughter, both the audience and my own, was the medicine I needed. Getting the last laugh took new meaning. I don't know if this pain is something I will continue to capitalize on, but it felt better rehashing it in a comedy club of three hundred friendly faces than to millions of strangers on TikTok. Maybe by the time you're reading this, I've found more consistent opportunities to make audiences giggle somewhere, somehow.

I declined New York Fashion Week invites for next week. As eye-roll-inducing as this declaration might sound, it's a big deal for the nasty little ego I had developed over the months since Beergate. It felt like I had to resort to looking hot and being seen instead of using my voice to keep my relevance alive. But I started pushing back against my ego, a hungry bitchy Tinker Bell type. I've learned that FOMO can be a powerful motivator when you use that time to execute something that will bring you even more joy later on. Fashion was taking a toll on my mental health. I could spend a week to get all dolled up in *Hunger Games* capitol clothing in an attempt to feel relevant, or I could stay home, write, see old friends, and sleep. Those events aren't going anywhere, and neither is my worth. When I look back on the last two years, fashion has been a key character. My memories are sorted not just by the days but by the outfits I wore. I wore the Hope Macaulay chunky knit sweater on Day 1. The Marchesa pink petal gown for Day 365. The Alice + Olivia Audrey dress in the Generic Beer ad. I made the *New York Times* Best Dressed list in my second year of womanhood. Maybe by the time you're reading this, I will have settled into my style and built a healthy relationship with my body image. My wardrobe is just getting started. But I *will* be keeping the tie-dye cat muumuu in my closet forever.

I sang a duet with Broadway icon Jessica Vosk in concert last week. I saw Jessica's last performance as Elphaba in *Wicked* while I was at the Cincinnati College-Conservatory of Music. If you would have told

me then that she would invite me to duet with her, I
would've thrown my shoe at you. We sang "Both Sides
Now," one of my favorite songs, a total transition
anthem. In musical theater, they say when a character
no longer has the words to express how they feel,
they start to sing. I haven't had the words lately,
but I've always found my voice through song. I'm
thinking about making a fun silly pop song about
girlhood to celebrate the joy I felt from the early
days now that I'm not so sad. More than anything,
though, I will always be a cringe musical theater girl
through and through. Maybe by the time you're reading
this, I'll have made my Broadway debut as a woman.
Unless I'm dead, I will be trying to get up there.

I kissed a gay man last week. We did a lot of kissing.
This initially felt wrong because I was scared of
how he viewed me. Did he see me as a man? Once I
let go of my own insecurities, I ended up feeling
really safe with him. I do believe we accept the
love we think we deserve, and I'm starting to
think that maybe that love could look a little different than I once imagined. My own desires and
attractions have evolved so much since the beginning
of my transition. I'd really like to let go of toxic
heteronormative romance and lean into the unknown.
Maybe by the time you're reading this I'll have the
hottest, sexiest, funniest boyfriend or girlfriend
or joyfriend (my pitch for nonbinary partners) and
we'll be super privately and publicly in love, in the
middle of planning to have our ayahuasca babies and

a televised wedding like that one psychic told me I'd have. How fun would that be! A girl can dream.

I haven't posted shitttt this week. I put so much energy into the internet, and I know my time with her is not over, but we are no longer monogamous. I will introduce her to my other girlfriends: writing, speaking, dancing, acting, singing. I think back to performing in *The Book of Mormon* and felt like the richest human in the entire world. The internet made me wealthy, and not once did I feel as rich or financially sound as I did when I was doing *The Book of Mormon*. I thought brands that paid me to promote their products were my forever friends; they weren't. I thought my followers were owed every detail of my life; they are not. I thought if only twenty people saw something and not twenty million, it was a failure; it is not. Maybe I needed to experience those twenty million views to know just how valuable twenty are. I liked the internet the most when every notification was a pleasant surprise and not an expectation. But what if it's the people who are still here, after the storm, who are the real wins? If I had any advice for someone who wanted to be a content creator, I would say enjoy every single day when you didn't go viral, because one day you will, and it will change your expectations of everything.

Maybe by the time you're reading this, TikTok no longer exists and it is merely a nostalgic memory to gen z. The thought of that makes me giggle. I do hope the words on this page will live longer than the videos I once made for TikTok.

I haven't had a dark thought yet this week. I'm starting to understand where they come from and why they became so loud. A lot of the dark thoughts were tied to my exhaustion.

When things felt too excessive and big, I wanted to run away.

When I read one too many hateful messages, I wanted to crawl under the covers and never come out.

When I didn't have the creative energy to live up to the expectations my ego had set for myself, I wanted to die.

Some of these dark thoughts could've been fought off by having courageous conversations with those around me. If I can't handle something, I need to ask for help. If I bite off more than I can chew, I need to cancel something. If there are too many external opinions, I need to step away from the phone. As for the other bad thoughts, well . . . I'm gonna go ahead and forgive myself because I was in some shitty situations. I did my best. It wasn't always enough. I'm still here. Maybe by the time you're reading this, my dark thoughts will be less frequent, and I hope yours are too.

And, last, I am reallllllly loving my womanhood lately. The euphoria of my femininity ebbs and flows, but it's always there, and it's always been there. Contrary to the contents of this book, I'm trying this new thing where I keep certain things to myself. Little yummy womanly moments just for me. Millions of people including politicians, journalists, celebrities, activists, moms, daughters, sisters, friends, and other dolls have projected their ideas of girlhood onto me, as I have onto them. At the end of the day, I am the one who truly knows what my gender journey has been and where it will go next. I cannot predict the full future (as much as I wish my overpriced psychics could), and I've filled these last pages with many maybes, but the one thing I can tell you for certain is that my soul is, always has been, and always will be a woman. Day 1 of my girlhood didn't begin when I came out just two years ago, but rather the day I took my first breath. And however that makes you feel, well, it's not really my business. I do hope it brings you joy and not pain. Maybe by the time you're reading this, trans and nonbinary people will be less hated and more loved. Maybe I will no longer feel like Public Enemy Number One. Maybe one day the dolls will transcend the two-dimensional projections of what society wants us to be and will be fully realized human beings as the women that we are and always have been.

Phew! Okay. I hope you had a good time. I sure did. We both deserve Domino's deep pan pizzas tonight.

LOVE YA,

Dylan

ACKNOWLEDGMENTS

Mom, thank you for meeting me halfway. May we always love and keep the conversation going.

Marina Shifrin, thank you for holding my hand through the writing of this book. I would dive into the creative deep end with you a million more times.

Sarah Robbins, thank you for taking a chance on this book, and giving me the time and grace to find exactly what it was supposed to be.

Diane Shaw, thank you for making this the most gorgeously designed book ever ever ever.

The rest of Team Abrams, **Lisa Silverman**, **Jenice Kim**, **Logan Hill**, and **Jodi Wong**, thank you for getting this book to the finish line.

Debora Szpilman, your illustrations bring this book to life—thank you for agreeing to every insane idea I had for them.

Gabby Fetters and **Alex Rice**, thank you for always leading with kindness and for believing in my writing abilities before I did.

Stacey, thank you for being the gentlest, kindest big sister a girl could ask for, and **Lulu**, for making a great addition to the fam.

Dad, thank you for your unwavering love, and **Jen**, thank you for loving my dad and me.

Mory Fontanez, thank you for showing me the value I have in this life, and reminding me when I can't see that myself.

Keeshlo, **Mae**, and **Annabel**, you are my chosen family. When life gets too scary, let's hop in a bathtub and say yes to the dress.

Our Lady J, thank you for teaching me when to stand my ground, and when to soften in this wild industry.

Lily, you got an entire dedication, but this is a specific thank-you for allowing me to write about your lady parts.

Steph, thank you for walking into the fire with me.

The women who glam me, **Laurel, Zenobia, Angie, Donnie, Kelly:** I love doing life with you.

Alok and **JVN,** thank you for the nonstop laughs and advice.

Mitch, thank you for matching my aesthetic. May we always find the cutest version of everything.

Benj and **Alex,** thank you for the brotherly protection and guidance you've given me.

Isabella and **Lexy,** thank you for being the dolls who showed me true sisterhood.

Alyah, thank you for seeing the "IT Girl" in me before anyone else did.

Meaghan, thank you for handling my craziness in stride, getting this book over the finish line, and being the ultimate yes woman.

The Trevor Project, thank you for being an absolutely iconic organization for queer youth, one we should all support.

Michele and **Andy,** thank you for bringing Lily into this world and for letting me practice my dance routines in your living room.

Josie and **Miss Benny,** for helping me feel young and reckless in the best ways.

The Hilton girls, for welcoming me into your lives and teaching me the true meaning of SLIVING.